FIFA Football

The Story Behind The Video Game Sensation

Lee Price

BENNION KEARNY

Published in 2015 by Bennion Kearny Limited.

Copyright © Bennion Kearny 2015

ISBN: 978-1-910515-39-6

Published by Bennion Kearny Limited
6 Woodside
Churnet View Road
Oakamoor
ST10 3AE

www.BennionKearny.com

Photo Credits

Sega Mega Drive, 3DO, Sega Saturn, PlayStation: Evan Amos; KSI relaxes at home: Jim Bennett; Bournemouth's Sylvain Distin undergoes the MoCap process: National Football Museum.

To my father, Gregg, who bought me my first games consoles – from the Mega Drive and PlayStation at Christmas to walking up that huge hill with the Dreamcast. You're at least partially responsible for this.

Thanks for inspiring me, and continuing to.

Lee Price

For almost as long as I can remember, I've loved football – and part of my fandom has manifested itself in video games related to the sport. The first I can remember playing was the slightly strange *Marko's Magic Football*, a side-scrolling platformer on the Sega Mega Drive, which bore little relevance to the game I adored – but I persevered with it anyway mainly because of the spherical object which occasionally appeared at the main character's feet.

With the PlayStation came my first taste of *FIFA*, and I was immediately hooked. I'd spend every resting minute of my day on *FIFA 97* – throwing hissy fits when I was told to come off the console before school, complaining I had an important match to play.

And, even then, I was writing books about *FIFA*. Although that consisted of scrapbooks filled with page after page of results and match reports from fictional leagues and competitions that I'd created and played out. There were also challenges and scenarios I had to fulfil – a notable one being using David Unsworth to score a goal at both ends of the pitch.

There were other games in-between – notably *Adidas Power Soccer*, *LMA Manager* and *Football Manager* – but *FIFA* always managed to rise above the parapet. The only one I've properly been unable to resist.

I fondly remember guiding Ireland to World Champion status in *FIFA: Road to World Cup 98*, and various sleepovers revolving around *FIFA* tournaments between *FIFA Football 2004* and *FIFA 07*, before University all-nighters took on a later, and boozier, dimension.

Now, as an adult – of sorts – the game still evokes that same primal response as real football, and is the go-to game for both my spare time, and evenings spent with my friends.

Looking at the front cover of this book, back at the history of the *FIFA* series, is so evocative – there are few media franchises with which you can track your entire life. This is an exception – seeing the year-by-year cover art is a nostalgic trip down memory lane, back to a simpler time in both football and video games, before returning to an age where both are huge commercial successes, and immensely powerful.

I enjoyed making that journey – and hope you do, too.

Lee

A little thank you to the people, without whom, there'd be no book

A big thank you to the following people for their help in putting this book together, by agreeing to be interviewed:

- Marc Aubanel for your enthusiasm.
- Rik Henderson for managing to reach back to 1993 so easily.
- Andy Bell for facilitating an interview with yourself rather than one of your many sports stars for me.
- Steven McKevitt for offering the fascinating perspective of a FIFA rival.
- Jan Tian for your honest and hilarious anecdotes.
- John Motson for being so readily helpful and living up to expectations as an idol.
- Gary Paterson for talking me through things I might never understand.
- Adam Hay and Paul Marr for taking me behind the scenes at EAC.
- Aaron McHardy, Santiago Jaramillo, David Rutter, Matt Prior, Nick Channon, Adam Shaikh, and Matt Jones for taking time out to speak to me while I was there – visiting just as *FIFA 16* stress levels hit maximum. Oops!
- Steve Schnur for beginning our chat before your morning coffee and toast.
- James Salmon, Nigel Nunn and Steve Cook for your help while at Bournemouth.
- Jack Wilson for supporting a rival tabloid writer.
- KSI for finding time in your busy schedule.
- Kay Murray for your speedy and informative replies.
- Chris Bullard and August Rosenmeier for sharing your World Champion experiences and expertise with me, and the readers.
- Rob Hodson for opening the FIFA community to me.
- Mark Lewington and Dave Howard at Game.

- Dan Bellis for allowing us inside FUTwiz.com.
- Ben Williams for talking me through your love for Ultimate Team.
- Nadia Gilani, Tom Bage and Katherine Sladden from Change.org.
- Drew Gibson for your games reviewer abilities.
- Matt Webster for fitting me in-between various flights – thank you.
- Dr Ian Pearson for taking me on a vivid journey into the future of video gaming.
- Jonathan Pile from ShortList for getting back to me so rapidly and keenly.

Finally, I should thank the key people behind the inception of this book – James Clifford and Sean Cotterell, of Clifford French, and Shaun White and Bryony Benoy at EA for believing in the idea and then making it happen; and my publisher James Lumsden-Cook for taking it on, despite the tight deadlines.

To Katherine Pease, for putting up with one-sided conversations and the emergence of my laptop as the third-wheel in our relationship – thank you. I owe you 100 hours of *Location, Location, Location*…

Foreword

I have a confession to make - once upon a time, I was a Pro Evo guy.

Back then, FIFA was just another football title. Which seems strange to think now.

That's because, since then, FIFA has come through like a steam train, taking over the genre as it came on in leaps and bounds.

With a killer combination of gameplay and realism, now there's only one game in the market - FIFA.

Today, it's the only game footballers talk about in the dressing room or on pre-season tours, wrangling over who's the FIFA champ at each club.

Which I am at mine - Beast Mode activated.

I don't hear of any 'rivals' to FIFA's crown now - I don't know anything about any other football games because, really, there aren't any.

That's because FIFA is the people's game, and the footballers' game, an institution in itself.

This book tells the story of the champ's rise, the people behind it, and the tech that powers the incredible graphics and gameplay.

Adebayo Akinfenwa

Table of Contents

Part One

Early Days
and The Making of a
Gaming Giant

Introduction

The greatest footballer in history stepped onto the stage, met by a standing ovation from a crowd of excited fans whooping and hollering for more than a minute. He waited patiently for them to get it out of their system; even for the sport's biggest icon, this was an extraordinary reception. Pele was used to adulating welcomes but, on this occasion, he was sharing the limelight.

Alongside him was David Rutter, a Mod-ish, fairly nondescript Englishman you might not recognise in the street, and the actual cause of the high voltage acclaim. Yes, it was cool that Pele was there, but Rutter's presence signalled that the main event of the day's conference was about to begin – they were going to talk about this year's *FIFA* game, *FIFA 16*.

When the applause finally died down, the downtown Los Angeles auditorium hushed and listened politely to the Brazil legend's anecdotes of how he coined the phrase 'joga bonito' or 'the beautiful game' – an amended version of which would soon be better known as the tag-line for EA Sports' latest release. But, really, the room was waiting on tenterhooks for tales of a different kind: what could they expect from the new *FIFA*?

Once a slightly baffled Pele was shuffled from the stage after a couple of minutes of engaging storytelling, the headline act began and the mammoth theatre fell silent in anticipation of news on the world's most popular sporting video game. Before a crowd of thousands of media from all around the world, with millions of fans watching at home via a live stream, Rutter began to outline some of the new elements of the hit series' latest release.

When he'd finished, he left the stage to an appreciative wall of noise – the audience's appetite suitably whetted by what was sure to be one of the best-selling games of all-time, *FIFA 16*. To an outsider, the topics discussed by Rutter would have seemed fairly general fare, but fans of the game were absorbed as he talked through some of the new features arriving to the series, while teasing them with hints of others yet to be announced. One thing was crystal clear from the producer's stint on stage: the new *FIFA* would be bigger and better than ever, which would make it something of a mammoth. Its predecessor, *FIFA 15*, had proved 2014's biggest selling game in the UK – selling a reported 2.66 million copies, 44.5% more than the second most popular game, that year's *Call of Duty: Advanced Warfare*, which sold 1.84 million units. Across all entertainment products, *FIFA* was second only to Disney sensation *Frozen* in Britain, while it also topped the biggest music album of the year, Ed Sheeran's *X*.

Globally, *FIFA 15* sold more than 15 million copies, around three times the figure achieved by stablemate *Madden NFL 15*, the game on which EA Sports was formed. *FIFA* is EA Sports' very own Pele.

The next day, at the E3 expo a short drive around the corner, *FIFA* was the centrepiece on EA's massive stand. As music pumped, lights flashed, and visitors flocked to join a queue to get hands-on with the game, footage of *FIFA 16* played out on a huge screen in the middle of it all. The trailer, narrated by the Brazil star, attracted more than seven million views online and starred football's biggest names.

On huge posters outside the *FIFA* room – inside which, excitable journalists would get to play the new game for the first time – Pele had been substituted. Lionel Messi, the greatest active footballer in the world and *FIFA* cover star, was now in prime position. This would be the first time anyone in the world outside of EA would get hands-on with the game. Those in attendance were prepared to wait hours to join that exclusive club. The queues outside the room remained constant, with only a set number of people allowed in per slot. Comfortably, it was one of the most popular booths at the entire show – despite E3's American setting and, therefore, reduced soccer fanbase.

*

Given its vast sales, *FIFA* has always been the EA Sports' highlight of the year. Indeed, the franchise accounted for 27% of EA's net revenues, and 23% of gross profits in 2013. And it's only getting bigger. Between 2010 and 2013, the units sold per instalment almost doubled from 6.4 million to 12.45 million. Since its first version was released in 1993, the series has sold more than 100 million copies worldwide. Last year's iteration, *FIFA 15*, became the most profitable video game in the world, generating £2.3 billion in sales – a figure *FIFA 16* will no doubt exceed.

This is thanks to an ever-expanding audience, as football continues its rapid rate of globalisation. In North America, where *FIFA*'s inception came in spite of scepticism from senior EA figures, in a territory that is traditionally ambivalent towards the sport, things are changing – *FIFA 15* was second only to *Madden* as the region's most popular sports video game, overtaking *NBA*, and shifting more than two million copies in the process.

That's incredible progress for a game that almost never was – which only survived having the plug pulled on it by being low budget and, therefore, low risk. While excuses were already being made for its anticipated failure, EA Sports found themselves stumbling upon the biggest sports franchise in the video game world.

As *FIFA 16* hits shelves across the globe, this is the story of the series from its very beginnings – how it emerged, and how it reimagined an entire genre of gaming.

1. Taking a toe-punt on 'soccer'
How FIFA Football nearly wasn't and then very suddenly was

In July 1993, modern football was adjusting to a new era. The first season of England's breakaway Premier League was underway, comprised of 22 clubs that had ditched the Football League for a share of a then-enormous TV deal.

Immediately, the influx of cash was felt, and footballers increasingly took on pin-up status. In that 1993 season, Alan Shearer had joined Blackburn Rovers for a British record £3.6 million, while the division's top scorer and Shearer's future international strike-partner, Teddy Sheringham, was signed by Tottenham for £2.1 million.

The inaugural campaign saw Manchester United crowned as English champions for the first time in 26 years, and their prodigious 19-year-old winger Ryan Giggs named as Young Player of the Year. The footballing landscape was all change – a period of history in the making.

With the £304 million splashed out by BSkyB and the BBC for five years of television rights, and highlights to the Premier League and the European Cup undergoing a similar rebranding that season (becoming the Champions League), football was to witness the introduction of a third new, major, game-changing franchise – the debut *FIFA* video game, entitled *FIFA International Soccer*, released in the aftermath of that seminal season.

It was Electronic Arts' (EA) first foray into the soccer video game market. Having established themselves in North America since 1988, with their first title – the American Football game *John Madden Football* – they wanted to break Europe. Research told them that it was the other football that would be their best bet.

The company had enjoyed success by securing official licenses to their American Football and Ice Hockey titles, so it was only natural that EA made a beeline for football's governing body, FIFA, negotiating a five-year deal. Though that sounds like a huge commitment, it was actually quite a tentative step. The agreement with FIFA included small royalty payments due to limited licensing: the first release didn't include any team or player names, logos or stadiums, or graphical likenesses. With a relatively small budget of $50,000 to $100,000 and a tiny team of just ten developers working on it, *FIFA International Soccer* was a toe dipped into the water rather than a bomb from the high board for EA.

EA Sports' roster of games was predominantly North American pre-*FIFA*.

Assistant Producer Marc Aubanel recalled that it was a low-risk punt into an unknown market, an experiment with something – soccer – they weren't really sure about. He said: "It really was an American company that had just started to have some success with the sport titles. Before EA Sports it was called EASN, Electronic Arts Sports Network, until ESPN sued and then they changed it.

"At that point in time, Europe was not a big market – they didn't even think FIFA was worth a franchise; were people going to buy it again and again?

"There was probably a concern that we were building a soccer game in Canada. I'm sure that was a bit strange for a lot of people. We had NHL right next to us and that seemed a much more natural fit.

"No one in San Francisco knew what FIFA was in fact, they pronounced it 'Fifer' when they saw it, and they couldn't understand why we were applying for a license when FIFA didn't run any league, just the World Cup."

Known initially as *EA Soccer*, the introduction of the moniker 'International' indicated the key licensing agreement – the only playable teams in the game were nations. Fictional squad lists took the place of real players. Instead of Shearer, Producer Matt Webster was England's striker; colleagues Joey Della-Savia (Italy) and Aubanel (France) lined up for their virtual national teams too, while Lead Producer Bruce McMillan put his newborn son into the game by way of tribute.

Nick Channon, now Senior Producer on *FIFA*, was beginning a career with EA at the time and remembers the release of the company's first football title with enthusiasm. He said: "I've been with EA for 23 years, working on the PGA games before we had the Tiger Woods license. I actually started in PR and took a journalist to Canada and, from that visit, that's how I ended up working on FIFA.

"EA Sports was very North American focused at the time, and here, all of a sudden, was a

European game. That felt *very* different, because it was all Madden and NHL at the time.

"You have to remember, it was an American company. In the last few years, football has become big in North America, and we've seen huge growth in our game, but back then, they didn't really know what it was. People would play football at a younger age, but it was never a big sport – the 1994 World Cup in the USA hadn't even happened at that time."

Though the game was coming out the season prior to a World Cup, EA were unable to make that a key element of their offering. The FIFA World Cup license belonged to a rival publisher, U.S. Gold, whose official game would be appearing on shelves in Spring 1994, in the build-up to America's hosting of the tournament.

Quite understandably, all these factors worried EA somewhat – the possibility of disastrous sales a very real one, with no clear USP to the game. In the midst of the confusion and alarm, it was briefly mooted that the game should be branded as *Team USA Soccer* in North America, to appeal to Americans' famous patriotism.

If more had been made of the World Cup rights issue earlier, it's a real possibility that EA could have pulled the plug on *FIFA* and changed the course of video game history. Sensibly, someone could have flagged it as an insurmountable obstacle, and the *FIFA* series might never have happened.

Marc Aubanel, who now works as a University lecturer, reflected: "It was a constant battle to not have it cancelled. Some games were committed SKUs (Stock Keeping Units), which meant that those titles were going to make X amount of revenue that fiscal year; or uncommitted SKUs, which were games where the approach was like 'well, we're spending some money on it but we don't know if it's ever going to ship'.

"FIFA was the latter, the sort of project that was done in a side room that no one knew about – it wasn't such an investment that people were panicking about it. It probably got put on the chopping block to be killed multiple times. Luckily, we were able to hide and get the game out before someone pulled the plug."

Thanks to the doggedness of the team working on the game – liaising across time zones between Canada and the UK – EA stuck to their guns, predicting healthy sales of 300,000 throughout Europe.

But their research was wrong. *FIFA International Soccer* hit the shelves in December 1993, a little over six months ahead of the World Cup and – crucially – before U.S. Gold's rival title. Within the first four weeks of sales alone, it had shifted half a million copies, instantly establishing itself as the biggest selling video game of the year – despite its December release – and it continued to top the charts for six straight months. As Channon put it: "It became quite a big game really quickly – it felt like FIFA was a big deal, even without all the licenses."

Aubanel added: "We doubled our sales forecast in the first five weeks, despite it shipping really late, so it was hugely successful. That cemented FIFA. We realised fairly soon that this series was going to run for a long time.

"Getting it out early was key. Timing is really important; you never want to be number two.

That was partly why FIFA became so popular and the official World Cup game didn't – when they came out, we were already out there and established."

U.S. Gold's *World Cup USA '94* was to be an irrelevance by the time it came out and was the last time the publisher secured the official FIFA World Cup franchise. That's because *FIFA International Soccer* was a revelation, reimagining the football video game genre. It was the first to step away from the norm of 16-bit graphics, with an isometric view of the pitch, rather than the bird's eye view best used by *Sensible Soccer*, or top-down angle that had also become popular at the time. This unique approach was inspired by a beach volleyball game created by British indie developers Jules Burt and Jon Law.

FIFA International Soccer earned rave reviews upon its debut, with *Edge* magazine highlighting the relationship between crowd noises and on-pitch action as particularly impressive. *GamePro* lauded the graphics and animation, while *Mega Machines Sega* hailed it as the "greatest soccer game yet seen".

The original *FIFA* team.

Back row, left to right: Jon Bruce, John Santamaria, Jan Tian, Linda Stansfield, Bruce McMillan, Joey Della-Savia, Lee Patterson, Jeff van Dyck, Kevin Pickell. Front row, left to right: David Adams, Brian Plank, Dianna Davies, Suzan Germic, Mike Smith. Not pictured: Marc Aubanel and George Ashcroft.

Rik Henderson was amongst those who reviewed the first release of the *FIFA* series, for Sky One's *Games World TV* and was an immediate convert. He said: "I was a massive FIFA fan right from the start – I've owned every single version of it through the years. The first one came out at a time when Sensible Soccer was king of the football games, because it was arcade-y and fast and in comparison, FIFA felt quite slow.

"But the thing that FIFA International Soccer had going for it was that it felt more like football, rather than just a game. Although it was nowhere near as sophisticated as it is now, even back then it felt more like football than anything else on the market."

Originally released for the Sega Mega Drive – the dominant console of the time – as *International Soccer*'s success became clear, EA ported it to other devices, including PC, Amiga, the SNES, and Game Boy.

FIFA's success was part of a ground-breaking time in video games – a year earlier, in 1992, fighter game *Mortal Kombat* had generated worldwide outrage for its gratuitous violence; SEGA's historic *Virtua Fighter* debuted in arcades two months before *FIFA*'s release; while 1994 was anointed as 'year of the cartridge' by Nintendo, as their Game Boy took gaming portable. The year's headlines were stolen by Sony in December, however, as they launched the iconic PlayStation, a year and a month after forming Sony Computer Entertainment.

In short, EA's timing in targeting the European market was impeccable. And who was the man they chose to lead the charge for the maiden title? Erm, David Platt. Then England's Mr Reliable, the playmaker had just completed a £5.2 million move from UEFA Cup winners Juventus to Italian rivals Sampdoria, and he was chosen as *FIFA*'s first ever cover star, in a photo showing him taking on Polish midfielder Piotr Świerczewski. Another version, for the later release on the SNES, showed Platt's Dutch Sampdoria teammate, Ruud Gullit, being beaten to a cross by Irish keeper Packie Bonner. In turn, the Goldstar 3DO release showed the US team's poster-boy, Alexi Lalas, winning a header against Norway, while the game itself boasted an array of improvements, including a rotating camera effect and enhanced graphics.

Such was the impact of *FIFA International Soccer,* a sequel was inevitable and, upon its release, *FIFA Soccer 95* was considered the established market leader, reflecting an incredible twelve months for EA Sports, as well as the team working on the game. As Marc Aubanel reminisces: "There was a massive shift in atmosphere after the first game's success.

"It was great to be vindicated – no one makes a game to die in obscurity – when we hadn't been getting a lot of positive responses from around us, and there was a lot of hesitance and negativity and doubts about even doing a sequel.

"The game just exploded, it seemed like we did every version under the sun. Some years we were doing like thirty or forty versions, if you think of all the different languages.

"It really allowed EA to enter into markets it may not have been able to with its other franchises. If you took out US sales, it was really the dominant game at the time, globally."

That second game, which went on sale in November 1994, for the Sega Mega Drive, saw the introduction of club sides from across eight different national leagues, including England's Premier League, Germany's Bundesliga, Italy's Serie A, Spain's La Liga, France's Ligue 1, and Holland's Eredivisie – although the squads still consisted of made-up players as the new licenses again didn't include real players. Penalty shootouts were the major gameplay addition, rather than the 'next goal wins' method used to decide drawn games in its predecessor.

FIFA Soccer 95's UK cover featured Tottenham goalkeeper Erik Thorstvedt, a member of Norway's World Cup squad – a slightly bemusing choice to the modern fan. The American version again featured Alexi Lalas (replete with magnificent beard and stylish hairband), seemingly the only recognisable soccer star in the States – helped by a sterling World Cup showing on home soil, which was, for many local viewers, a first taste of the sport.

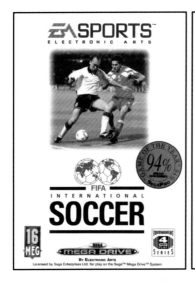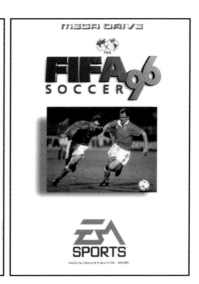

The first three covers of the *FIFA* series.

Subsequent editions also featured some surprise choices for cover star – which is now a sought-after position, as evidenced by the social media campaign to vote for who would join Lionel Messi on the UK edition of *FIFA 16*. Jordan Henderson eventually succeeded, seeing off England teammate Harry Kane, despite the Tottenham striker urging his fans to vote for him, and support coming from *Match of the Day* pundit Alan Shearer, boxer David Haye, and snooker player Ronnie O'Sullivan. Winner, Henderson, tweeted his joy at the result, the Liverpool captain writing: "Proud to have won the vote to be on the cover of *FIFA 16*."

In 2015, the *FIFA* cover is seen as prime real estate for image rights and building a footballer's global profile and brand. Sports PR expert Andy Bell, of The Sports Partnership – who manage various stars, including 2009 Formula 1 world champion Jenson Button, Olympic Boxing heavyweight gold medallist Anthony Joshua, and two-time NBA All-Star Luol Deng – said: "There is no doubt that being named a cover star for *FIFA* is a huge deal for individual footballers; it is almost a rite of passage from a recognised player to global superstar. Not to mention the bragging rights it gives individual players who all love playing the game!

"For instance, in 1998 EA used an image of David Beckham on the *FIFA* cover. There is no doubt that that would have been another piece in the puzzle which led Beckham to be, arguably, the most marketable footballer on the planet. His image on the cover, in a World Cup year, would have shown a whole raft of potential sponsors and brands that he had everything in terms of marketability.

"Being on the cover certainly shows to other brands the individual footballer in question has a very marketable presence which, if harnessed correctly, can generate a huge amount of revenue for the player. The gaming market is very interesting as, unlike other industries, such as music for example, the physical product cannot be pirated or shared illegally; therefore, the physical product is sold in droves – with the player's image walking into millions of people's homes.

"The game makers are very smart with the cover as it is a publicity moment within its own right. The growth of social media has allowed them to bring fans into the mix on who should be selected to be on the cover, generating a huge amount of pre-launch publicity."

Back in the early years, though, it took a while for that status to be realised. *FIFA 96*, for instance, saw Frank de Boer joined by Jason McAteer – the newly signed Liverpool midfielder, seemingly only chosen as he happened to appear alongside reigning Champions League winner de Boer in an international clash between Holland and Ireland.

FIFA 97 featured Newcastle's French winger David Ginola in full flow on their European cover art, while the rest of the world were treated to ageing Brazil star Bebeto. It wasn't until the following year, with the release of *FIFA: Road to World Cup 98*, that the cover star started to become more obvious – that edition kept Ginola for the French version but also boasted David Beckham (UK), Raul (Spain), Paolo Maldini (Italy) and Andreas Möller (Germany).

This was yet another example of savvy marketing from EA Sports, using their expensively assembled licenses to drive sales and exert their dominance in the market. This was a new era of consumerism – a standard global cover wasn't going to cut it (something EA were onto first). As Marc Aubanel explains: "It's hard to find a player who's not divisive, who's going to work in Germany, Italy, Spain, England and not have one country say 'we hate that team/player'.

"So Beckham was a big deal, but no more so than Maldini or Raul. Each was valuable to their region. In 1998, we were trying to maximise the sales in each country. We were shipping a separate version to each country anyway, so why not have different players on the cover? You couldn't take British games and move them to the Spanish shops, so we could localise to that market.

"There are very few players that transcend the sport and don't become regional heroes that are negative figures in other countries."

Ginola and Beckham helped EA Sports to 'wing' over new fans.

FIFA 99's worldwide cover star was Dennis Bergkamp, the stand-out player from the previous summer's World Cup, while the UK versions of the next three titles featured bonafide Premier League stars Sol Campbell (*FIFA 2000*), Paul Scholes (2001) and Thierry Henry (2002). It was in 2003, as the series skyrocketed, that the familiar line-up of a trio of footballing juggernauts was debuted, with Roberto Carlos, Ryan Giggs and Edgar Davids the three selected. Landon Donovan replaced Carlos in the States. *FIFA Football 2004* had Henry teaming up with Alessandro Del Piero and Ronaldinho; 2005 featured Patrick Vieira alongside Fernando Morientes and Andriy Shevchenko, before Wayne Rooney and Ronaldinho shared four straight covers.

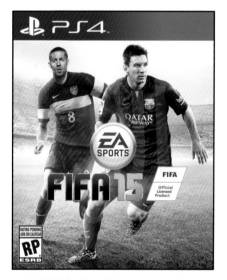

International success: the French cover of *FIFA 07*, with domestic star Juninho added; while the American version of *FIFA 15* saw Clint Dempsey called up.

By *FIFA 10*, virtually every region had a different line-up on its cover, with Rooney a regular feature, appearing alongside international teammates Frank Lampard and Theo Walcott in the UK, before playing sidekick to Real Madrid star Kaka on *FIFA 11*, for which the Brazilian was the global face. *FIFA 12* was a similar mash-up, Rooney, again prominent, was joined by Arsenal midfielder Jack Wilshere in the UK.

It was *FIFA 13*'s cover that confirmed the value of the cover star berth, though, when it was announced that Lionel Messi – previously the face of rival game *Pro Evolution Soccer* – had signed to front *FIFA* globally.

He has been doing so ever since. In the diminutive Argentine, EA had finally settled upon a cover athlete who could match the longevity offered by Tiger Woods and their *PGA* series of golf games. Indeed, the American megastar fronted the game between 1998 and 2013, before passing on the baton to Rory McIlroy.

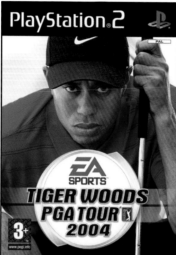

Tiger Woods set the benchmark for a cover-star across a series.

EA's thirst for licenses is best exemplified by the experiences of Steven McKevitt, who was Head of PR at Gremlin Interactive during the Nineties, and worked on *Actua Soccer*, a would-be rival to *FIFA*.

He said: "Actua Soccer was one of the launch titles for the PlayStation in 1995, and it was really advanced – the first 3D football game and the first to use motion capture. It also had a really advanced commentary engine. So, in about 90% of the reviews, it did better than FIFA, which still hadn't really cracked 3D at that point. In spite of that, we didn't sell as many as EA. Even then, FIFA was a juggernaut – but we knew EA had been stunned; they even tried to poach a few people on the team.

"While we were working on Actua Soccer 2, the opportunity to get the Premier League license came up. Both EA and ourselves went for it, along with Eidos, who made Championship Manager. With hindsight, I think there was a slight degree of complacency on our side. A few people thought that because we were a British company, that could cut some ice with the Premier League – 'well, EA are American, they call it soccer, it's developed in Canada, so what do they know?' – that sort of thing.

"We put a lot of effort into the pitch, though, and we had good support from people involved in the game – Trevor Brooking, the Match of the Day commentator Barry Davies, and quite a few of the Premier League clubs as well.

"Surprisingly, the FA didn't immediately award the license to anyone following the pitches. A few months of negotiations followed before they announced that they were giving it to EA.

"By the time Actua Soccer 2 came out, it was clear that EA were catching up and, the following year, when Actua Soccer 3 was released, they'd so completely eclipsed us that it was game over for Actua.

"The thing that most impressed me about EA was how much they learned from the competition. They weren't just resting on their laurels because they'd got the Premier League license; they really just wanted to have the best game. It's that combination of investment in the R&D side, a real understanding of what fans want and supporting that with licenses. That's made them unstoppable.

"We were delighted when the original Actua 'beat' FIFA, but that's where it ended. Rather than use that to take subsequent games to the next level, we squeezed three versions out of the same engine. Meanwhile, EA were committed to improving everything on all fronts. We were too dismissive to learn from EA, and that was the difference between the two companies – if you asked people at Gremlin what they thought of FIFA or even Pro Evo, quite a few would say 'rubbish'. EA didn't think we were rubbish, they learned from what we had done, and then tried doing it much better.

"You only had to look at EA Sports. At a time when games of questionable quality were released all the time, they never seemed to put out a bad game. EA had that attention to detail. 'If it's in the game, it's in the game' wasn't just a strapline, it was something they committed to.

"Working on PR for Actua Sports, I ended up feeling just completely under-gunned, like leading cavalry into battle against panzers. At Gremlin, we knew how to make games – but EA knew how to build franchises."

Gremlin weren't the only ones to feel like they were off the *FIFA* pace in the early nineties – it took EA Sports' hunger for official licensing to spark the English FA and Premier League into life on what would, later, be a hugely lucrative route. Back in 1993, 'image rights' wasn't a recognised phrase, let alone a standard contract clause – so EA Sports actually played a major part in formalising such detail in English football, when they were trying – unsuccessfully – to secure them.

Tom Stone, who worked on *FIFA* in the UK team, told *MCV* in 2013: "My first job at EA was to get on a plane and fly to Switzerland to see FIFA. We met the head of ISL Marketing who were the representatives of FIFA, and we shook hands on a deal there and then over dinner. The deal lasted through until 1998; it was a five-year deal. I'm not going to reveal what the royalty payments were, but they were miniscule.

"In many ways, our asking for these rights helped football become organised. I went to the Football Association, the Premier League, the PFA and so on. I got to know these people quite well and they were like, 'Oh, right, who has the rights to player likenesses then? Who has the rights to the stadium? These guys are asking for those rights.' So, in a way, we actually helped the associations work all these things out."

Not that EA Sports were the experts on all things licensing – though they secured the rights to eight national leagues for *FIFA Soccer 1995* in that deal, they didn't manage to negotiate rights for any of the players in those divisions. Oops!

*

Gameplay and stature have come a long way from the series' beginnings. Lead Programmer on *FIFA International Soccer* was Jan Tian – probably better known as Janco Tianno the Brazil forward, his in-game alter ego – and he remembers laying the foundations of *FIFA* clearly.

He said: "I came to Canada from China in the early Eighties, when I was about 30. I got into gaming by accident, because it wasn't an industry back then. I was working in the computer hardware field when my recruiter suggested a vacancy at a game company, and I said 'what's a video game?' That company went on to be bought by EA.

"At the time of FIFA International Soccer, I had just finished a tennis game, and my manager wanted me to work on this project because I played soccer. They gave me a little prototype and it had the isometric view of a player dribbling a ball. There was no gameplay but it had something; it was different. So I went out and bought every soccer game in the store, and wrote reviews on each of them, the good and the bad.

"From that, I started to make my own prototype. I drew the field, without goalposts, the ball was a white dot and players were just a vertical line. Once I had worked out how to dribble a ball, I put five players on the field and started to work on AI. That was the major challenge.

"Player versus player is fine, there's no challenge, but for someone to sit at home and play a computer is. But computers were really weak back then, with not a lot of memory and there was no graphics card.

"Other sports games were assuming the position of a super-coach, directing the game like a show – you go there and you go there. But that's not how soccer works. The most important thing in soccer isn't shooting or passing, it's positioning, where to stand. The digital process of 22 players doing that would need a lot of power, more than we had. So I created a formation table technology to speed up a team's logic."

Single-handedly, Tian had created the template for the series to follow for years to come, effectively creating, from scratch, the *FIFA* game we know and love today. For the first month of the project he worked alone, until he turned to his colleagues – who were busy with other projects – for some feedback.

"I asked my co-workers to come try it. We started playing and got a game going. They were standing at the table, cheering, like a real soccer game. At that point, I knew we had something.

"One of the senior, senior execs happened to be walking past and saw us playing the prototype and said: 'Oh, this game has to ship before Christmas.' My original estimate was 13 months. I was like 'shit', so we formed a small team really quickly – two or three engineers and a couple of artists – but a really great team, and got to work."

With the stakes suddenly raised by the massively reduced turnaround time, plus the pressure of seeing off the rival U.S. Gold title, the team had to work around the clock to make *FIFA International Soccer* viable.

Jan chuckles: "Those first two *FIFA*s, holy smoke, I almost killed myself. I worked myself into the hospital emergency room three times, I was that exhausted. My kids were still very little back then. For a couple of months, I didn't see them. One day, I was working late on a Sunday night, just me and my manager Bruce McMillan, when the phone rang.

"He answered it, and it was my son – he said: 'Could you please let my dad come home, please?' That almost brought Bruce to tears. But that was how hard I worked – nobody forced me to, I was just so passionate about what I wanted to do. We were fortunate, really. To take on a game by yourself now – there's no way, people don't give you that chance. We realised that.

"And EA were always fantastic with us. For example, during those two games, I don't remember which exactly, my dad had his first stroke, and he lived in Beijing in China. EA bought me the airline ticket and said, 'Jan, go back to see your dad for two weeks, don't worry about work'. So I flew back with my wife and kids, with my daughter on my passport, because you can have two people on the same visa.

"After a week, my dad had mostly recovered, and I was thinking so much about FIFA that, at that first weekend, I decided I had to go back. I had tasks to finish. Back then, there weren't that many flights from Beijing to Vancouver, so you couldn't change.

"In order for me to get a plane home early, I had to go to the airport with my sister, holding a bag of $1,000 to try and bribe someone she knew on the crew desk to get me a flight.

"Isn't that crazy? I did it, but I'd forgotten that my daughter was still on my passport – two weeks later, she couldn't leave China. My wife had to struggle in China for another month, until the Canadian Embassy could get her another passport and get her out.

"To this day, I can't believe that I did that. But it's the sort of story I will tell my grandchildren one day; a highlight, in a way."

Amongst those anecdotes of dedication and self-sacrifice, surely, is the success story that *FIFA* has gone on to become, building on Tian's solid starting point. The programmer, now working at Microsoft, is incredibly modest about his achievements, saying: "I'm so proud of what my team achieved and what FIFA has become – I feel like, finally, I contributed something to the gaming industry.

"It's great that it gave so many young people so much joy and happiness, that's all that matters, to be honest. After so many years, people are still interested in the story of FIFA – people always ask me about it. I'm happy they remember it as a great game."

With the game developing rapidly and dramatically, it did not take long for *FIFA* to become unrecognisable compared to its original release…

**Jan Tian receiving EA's Outstanding Performance Award
from executives Don Mattrick and Bing Gordon, for his work
on *FIFA International Soccer*.**

From McAteer to Messi and 2D to motion capture imagery

The development of the *FIFA* video game series since its inception in 1993, if sketched, would probably resemble something like the 'evolution of man' image, but with a ball at the character's feet.

So how exactly did the game go from a new entry in the crowded football game market, to the all-conquering, globally recognised brand that generates millions? Here, with the help of a few experts and gameplay images sourced from EA Sports, we track that journey game-by-game, highlighting the key developments, introductions and innovations.

FIFA International Soccer | **Released: December 1993**

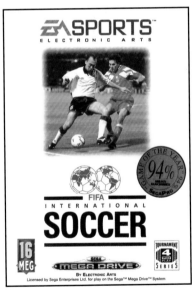

The first *FIFA* certainly made an unexpected splash, as we explored in Chapter One, with Lead Programmer Jan Tian recalling fondly: "We had no idea how big the game would be. To be honest, back then, a project was a project.

"But I felt passionate about it because it was something I liked to play – and I was not a typical gamer. My managers in the company gave me the authority to design the gameplay however I wanted it to be. I had freedom to create a game for myself.

"It started to build in momentum, people really liked it and I could feel it. I liked it, my team liked it, the testers, the QA people, they all liked it. You know when you've got something good.

"The sales figures for the first month were unheard of back then, it was incredible. I actually got an award – the Outstanding Award – from EA for that. If I'd known that I was working on something that would turn out to be this great, I don't know how I would've felt."

However, though that first title was to prove historic and revelatory, it wasn't without its imperfections, something even the enthusiastic Tian readily admits: "There was a lot that I wasn't happy with on the first game, but we had to finish it when we did. I could've spent a lot longer on it."

For games journalist Rik Henderson, his affection for the newcomer was bittersweet: "The isometric view made it stand out, but it was also the problem with the game – I seem to remember it having sweet spots from where you could score almost every single time.

"It was very much a case of 'now go left, now go right, hit the ball from outside the area' and it will go into the top corner. It was an inauspicious start. FIS was a very slow game. Over the years, the PES/FIFA debate has raged but, in FIFA's early days, it didn't hold a candle to any of its peers. It took quite a while for it to come through.

"The first breakthrough for FIFA was the re-release of FIS on the 3DO console, because up to then the 16-bit games were very much similar. The 3DO version came along and introduced a more 3D aspect to the game, and certainly better graphics – it's just that nobody bought a 3DO!"

And those inside EA Sports, too, were particularly fond of the new 3DO console, not least because former colleague Trip Hawkins was establishing the brand. The platform may not have proven to be a success, but it helped to demonstrate the future of the *FIFA* series, as Marc Aubanel reveals: "The favourite game I worked on was the 3DO version of FIS. It was a game that EA constantly contemplated killing. It was only really made as a favour to Trip.

"But it was our first attempt at doing 3D, it was really exciting and it was the first time many of us had seen 3D models. We had complete freedom to make the game. There were no sales associated with it – it really wasn't a big deal.

"But as soon as people saw the demo, everyone said, 'This is where EA Sports is going'. We made the very first 3D prototype of a sports game in the world. When the Madden team saw it, they wanted to follow us, which was exhilarating – we were really out in front of the curve."

FIS, despite being a basic dive into soccer simulation, offered four different modes – Exhibition, Tournament, Playoffs and League. Of these, Tournament was the virtual representation of the World Cup, the event EA couldn't secure the license to.

Similarly, Playoffs also took users into the midst of an international tournament, but parachuted them straight into the knockout stage.

In all, 48 national teams were represented in *FIS*, plus the EA All Stars, with every squad consisting of 20 players – all of whom looked the same, barring different skin tones.

Famously, *FIS* contained a glitch that would become video game legend. A player could get a tap in by standing in front of the opposition's goalkeeper when he was about to kick the ball from his hands.

The game, despite its superb marketing and licensing, had a tagline that could have done with some more polish: "FIFA International Soccer has it all... experience sheer brilliance." Catchy.

FIFA Soccer 95 | Released: November 1994

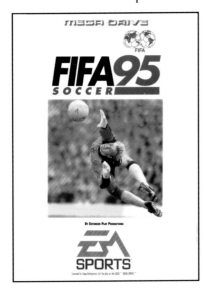

After such a feted debut, would second album syndrome kick in for EA Sports' fledgling franchise? After all, much of their initial impact had been the result of a standout view – the novelty of which surely would have worn off by now – and having the *FIFA* branding, but none of the players.

Both elements remained but with one crucial introduction to spice things up – the licenses for eight major leagues around the world were secured. The full leagues included were the English Premier League, France's Ligue 1, Germany's Bundesliga, Serie A in Italy, Holland's Eredivisie, and the Spanish La Liga.

Some teams were also taken from Brazil and the American Professional Soccer League, the US's second division.

It wasn't definitive by any means but, slowly, it was getting there in terms of realism.

'*FIFA 2*', as it was known inside EA, became a commercial success like its predecessor, earning positive critical reviews too, which must have been a relief to the team working on it, given the sudden expectations of greatness.

Or not, as Jan Tian recalls: "For FIFA 2, people always ask if I had a pressure on me, but I don't remember having any. There were a few things I wasn't happy about from the first one, because it was rushed, like the header and the AI – the goalkeeper logic is very difficult to write – so I improved on them.

"The code I wrote for the first two games was used for FIFA for many years after I left (following FIFA Soccer 95). The big change for FIFA 2 was the one-touch passing. That was tough, because it was either 0 or 1 – you pressed or you didn't. Now, it has passing of different power based on how long you hold it for, so that's something we introduced."

Penalties replaced the playground style next-goal-wins decider at the end of extra time in *FIS*. Curiously, despite the initial success of its predecessor, this was the only game in the main *FIFA* series not to be released on more than one platform, with EA opting only to put the game out on the Sega Mega Drive. The game's tagline was snappier than *FIS*'s, though. It was: "The best console football can get".

There was still a sense of work to be done, though, as most of the divisional line ups in the game were based on the season just passed - rather than the season ahead, as *FIFA* games now operate.

FIFA Soccer 96 | **Released: September 1995**

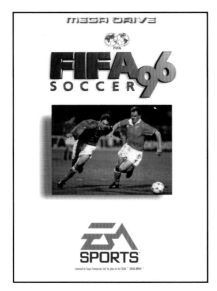

Though the SNES and Mega Drive releases used the *FIFA 95* engine for gameplay, *FIFA 96* was a huge leap forward for the series – and was possibly a pivotal moment.

EA Sports' timing, as ever, was perfect. With the forerunner of future rival *Pro Evolution Soccer: Goal Storm* released just months later, they made another crucial breakthrough in licensing. *FIFA 96* was the first in the series to secure licensing for player names.

This, combined with team names and leagues – with the Scottish Premiership added alongside Sweden's Allsvenskan and Malaysia's Super League – would maintain *FIFA's* appeal in a crowded market. As Rik Henderson raves: "The reason why FIFA, for me, has always been the number one football game – and for genuine football fans, rather than just gamers – is because it's always had the licenses and the kits.

"There's nothing worse than playing as the Anfield Reds on PES; that used to wind me up. I had to change all the team names and rename every player in the game. So FIFA having the licenses is a huge deal, and they got in really early for them."

However, it wasn't quite perfect immediately – the Brazilian teams in the game featured various discrepancies, with long-retired players included on squad lists, while the American league remained fictitious, with MLS just a few months old. Generally, though, and especially for the European market, it signalled another huge leap forward.

Assistant Producer Marc Aubanel recalls licensing, more than anything else, being EA Sports' biggest focus for the early years of the *FIFA* series – the publisher investing heavily to corner what they considered a crucial market. He said: "As soon as the first version came out and it was successful, EA just put its weight and effort into getting licenses for soccer – which, at the time, was not trivial.

"In North America, it was a one-stop shop – for Major League Baseball, you'd go to the players' association and the league. It's two meetings and you get a game licensed. With soccer, it was years and hundreds of meetings to get the licenses.

"We spent an inordinate amount of money and time to get those licenses; it cost us a lot of our bottom line because soccer is so large and complicated. From a business standpoint, that was the biggest challenge, and the biggest threat to the franchise was – what if someone else got an exclusive license with Manchester United, what if we lost the biggest team in the world?

"We went to FIFPRO, we went to the teams, we went to the leagues, it was quite a complex affair to get all of those licenses – but I think that gave us at least a few years' legs-up on our competition.

"It was clear, even in those early days – with the improved graphics on the horizon that we'd seen on the 3DO dev kits – that we were going into an era of poly-realistic gaming, and the licenses, therefore, were key."

Licensing wasn't the only thing that impressed at a timely moment. As well as the emergence of rival *PES*, this was the first *FIFA* to be released on the groundbreaking new platform, the PlayStation.

With Sony's console set to become virtually ubiquitous – and change the video game industry forever – EA Sports were amongst those to capitalise first on the power on offer, bravely moving away from the isometric viewpoint that had done so much to establish the brand and moving into real-time 3D graphics, with their 'Virtual Stadium' technology. Having seen the success of the 3DO release of *FIFA International Soccer*, they worked on developing that technology, and it was ready just in time to make a big splash.

Henderson continues: "It was a fun game that everyone enjoyed on the SNES, but it wasn't the dominant force on that console. I think the first instance where FIFA made people sit up and take notice of it was when it first came out on the PlayStation One.

"It became, very rapidly, *the* football game for PlayStation. It took it away from the isometric viewpoint and gave it a more free-flowing, TV-style approach, and that really helped. I think it needed the extra graphics part for it to finally reach some kind of dominance. Previously, FIFA was seen as a slower, more simulation-based game than some of its rivals."

Also added for the first time in the series were positions, rankings, transfers, team customisation tools, and a proper introduction sequence. Possibly most significant, though, was the addition of a soundtrack – 15 songs composed and arranged by Graeme Coleman. This was to pave the way for a huge part of how *FIFA* has become so culturally pervasive, with future playlists becoming as sought-after as airplay on Radio One. In 2015, *FIFA* is the music streaming service used by many gamers.

Another first for *FIFA 96* was that it was the first in the series to have a proper, formal introduction sequence at the start of the game. This would be something that would be built upon as the game developed – with *FIFA*'s presentation one of the distinguishing elements when compared to rivals.

FIFA 97 | **Released: October 1996**

Building on the successful introduction of Virtual Stadium, and using the recognised and established *FIFA* practice of introducing and defining improvements in one game, then refining them in the next, *FIFA 97* upgraded the 2D 'sprites' that represented players, replacing them with polygonal characters, accentuating the 3D impact.

This was helped by a first dabble in motion capture, undertaken by European cover star David Ginola, although this didn't mean every player in *FIFA 97* was quite as silky with the ball at their feet as the Frenchman, sadly.

But the biggest improvement of the match day presentation was aimed not at the gamer's eyes, but at their ears – as a real-life team were recruited to front *FIFA* coverage. The game's commentators were John Motson of the *BBC*, and Andy Gray of *Sky Sports*, with then *Match of the Day* host Des Lynam the presenter.

In an interview for this book, Motson revealed that the offer from EA Sports was a surprising one, but he welcomed their decision to headhunt him, going after the game's 'official' voice, as it were, just as they'd sought out licenses for teams and players previously.

He said: "I was bemused at first because I didn't know anything about computer games. My son, of course, played the game so it was well known to me and my family at the time, so I wasn't sceptical – I knew they had the germ of an idea, and it was at a time when football was becoming fashionable again: the Premier League hadn't long started, and ideas were coming forward to exploit and market football in different ways.

"Clearly, Electronic Arts was a company that was going places – having made their name with Ice Hockey and other North American sports titles – and they wanted to get in on the ground floor of football computer games.

"I remember going into a studio in London, not knowing what to expect, with two guys from Canada who didn't really know what they wanted. They had a very limited list of names, and they said, 'could you shout a few phrases with excitement?'

"So I was sitting there in the studio shouting things like 'goal' or 'what a close miss'. It was so primitive; you would never have believed what it would grow into."

Motson worked on the game for several years, from the early stages right through until the *FIFA* series was an established juggernaut, and he offers more insight into the commentary process in Chapter Five.

Not that it was always a well-oiled machine. Given that it was early days for in-game commentary, it didn't always go to plan – *FIFA 97* became famous for some of its amusing mishaps: including a goal in the first minute being described as "that would win it surely".

Brilliant!

FIFA 97 featured six modes, including a six-a-side indoor option, while multiplayer games were an option for the first time, with up to 20 players via LAN, or eight via modem. This exploratory delve into online multiplayer would be a key element of what would go on to shape the series – now, the majority of single-player matches played on *FIFA* are online.

FIFA: Road to World Cup 98 | **Released: November 1997**

A massively significant release in the *FIFA* series, incorporating various key elements that would become standard for future iterations. Perhaps most notably, the game was the most marketable and culturally significant.

A triumvirate of major breakthroughs included an official soundtrack made up of real artists and songs – the title track, Blur's *Song 2*, becoming the band's biggest hit in the US, and almost synonymous with *FIFA 98*. Although the band needed a bit of persuading to allow their song on the game, that initial scepticism was won over by the offer of World Cup Final tickets.

Getting the band on board, though, was another marketing breakthrough for the series, once again setting the standard across the video game industry. Marc Aubanel remembers: "There was an EA game called Road Rash, which licensed music, but they paid a royalty on the songs, which was expensive, so Larry Probst, President of EA at the time, put a ban on licensing music. He said, 'we can't lose another X number of percentage points to music, this is crazy, we should keep writing our own music like we have since day one'.

"Before I was at EA, I worked in TV, and no one on radio or TV in the US paid royalties, so we tried to just negotiate a flat fee. We went to Blur, and they'd never heard about the Road Rash deal, and I think we got the song for something like $5,000; it was just an absolute steal in terms of how little it was.

"I remember when we went to the boardroom to present the game, we put on Song 2 and Larry immediately recognised it and said, 'That's not going in the game, is it?' I thought he was going to kill us, he started to freak out, but we told him about the deal and he calmed down – it was cheaper than hiring someone to compose our own song. How do you turn down Blur for five grand?

"FIFA 98 was a bit of a switching point where people wanted to be a part of the game – people were coming to us rather than the other way around. That was roundabout the time we had the CDs and we realised we had lots of room on the disc; in fact, we were running out of ideas of what to put on the disc, so music just seemed like a natural extension.

"And music and sports just go hand-in-hand – during TV commercials and all the stoppages in NFL, and in the stadium itself, there's music playing."

The other major steps taken for *Road to World Cup 98* were having David Beckham as the UK cover star and, crucially, earning the licenses to the World Cup and all 172 FIFA-registered national teams – something EA Sports had coveted for their first release. Now, the *FIFA* series was official. On this, Aubanel adds: "We wanted the previous World Cup title, in 1994, but we were way too late, so it was important to get it for 1998.

"And man, did that game sell! It was a massive success for us, and we were really nervous, because we'd only had six months to work on it. It ended up being a product that everyone was really proud of."

The team's pride wasn't misplaced. It was the most definitive football game released yet, with a massive amount of detail that was lapped up by consumers. It built up to the France World Cup the following summer with the Road to World Cup mode, which took users back to the start of qualifying if they wished.

Domestically, 189 club sides were playable, while the offside rule – previously a bugbear for many – was rectified, as EA Sports delivered an impressive game all-round. With the growing dominance of the PlayStation, *FIFA 98* was the last to be released on the 16-bit consoles that the series started on, such as the Mega Drive and SNES.

FIFA 99 | **Released: November 1998**

Given the success of its predecessor, *FIFA 99* was a little more low-key. Inspired by the popularity of the wealth of playable teams in *Road to World Cup 98*, EA Sports expanded the club pool to 205 playable sides including, for the first time, a 'Rest of Europe' block, which is now commonplace as 'Rest of World'.

The major introduction here was the European Dream League, building on the idea of a breakaway division of the continent's elite clubs, while graphically, basic facial animations were added, as well as other cosmetic specifics such as height, kits and emblems, as EA Sports, not content with just the licenses, strove to make every element of their game instantly recognisable. The title track was another inspired choice – Fatboy Slim's *The Rockafeller Skank*.

The indoor mode from previous games was scrapped, but the sense of that mode lived on in a noted improvement to gameplay fluidity, and responsiveness. *FIFA* was also starting to generate more response in the online world, with a large number of websites cropping up surrounding the game, run by fans of the game.

FIFA 2000 | **Released: October 1999**

Another year of experimentation from EA Sports, trialling features that would become familiar to fans of the series. This time, it was the inclusion of more than 40 classic teams, filled with legendary former players.

Also, perhaps more significantly for the company at the time, *FIFA 2000* was the first to boast the license for Major League Soccer – something geared towards the lukewarm American market.

Following *FIFA 99*'s demoing of facial animations, a new engine was used for 2000, adding more detail and animations, with looks suddenly very important for the *FIFA* makers. It was also the first *FIFA* to allow players the ability to play over consecutive seasons, with promotion, relegation and European qualification all on offer.

Along with new national leagues from Denmark, Greece, Israel, Norway and Turkey, EA Sports also added English League One side Port Vale to the game – part of their payment to Valiants' fan Robbie Williams to have his song, *It's Only Us*, as the theme music.

This was a significant release, as new rival *Pro Evolution* had emerged six months earlier. The series formerly known as *Winning Eleven* was rebranded as *ISS Pro Evolution*, including club sides for the first time, and earning rave reviews, such as a 97% from *Play Magazine*, who dubbed it 'the best football game [they] have ever seen'.

FIFA 2001 | **Released: November 2000**

Another iteration, another graphics engine, as the series came to the new PlayStation 2 but, this time, some players had their own unique faces. What might seem trivial now – when players are instantly recognisable in-game – was a huge leap for any football video game at the time.

Another debutant was the licenses for official club emblems for the first time, as EA continued their thirst for official status in every way possible.

That search for realism also brought a 'hack' button – a tap of the R1 button – enough to send your defender into a flying sliding tackle. Though it was popular amongst fans of the series – although, often, for comical reasons rather than enhancement of the gameplay – it didn't return in future editions.

2001 was the first in the series with a power bar for shooting – though the SNES version of FIS had something similar, it was exclusive to that platform – and, for music fans, Moby's *Bodyrock* was the title song.

Graphics from an early *FIFA* release – *FIFA 01* – with Manchester United star Paul Scholes just about identifiable.

FIFA Football 2002 | Released: November 2001

Given their success in 2001, power bars were introduced for passing, fully customisable for gamers who wished to fine-tune their control preferences.

More than a decade before Ultimate Team's introduction, EA Sports had a card reward system licensed – yes, another license – from Panini, which encouraged gamers to complete different competitions, with the offer of special 'star player' cards as reward for doing so.

The first to feature the word 'football' in the title, 2002 was to be the last *FIFA* game for more than a decade with a solo cover star – fronted by Thierry Henry – until Lionel Messi's EA Sports' deal started with *FIFA 13*.

Also bidding the series sayonara was the Japanese national team – with their Football Association agreeing to sell its exclusive rights to rivals Konami, the makers of *Pro Evolution Soccer*, during 2002. *FIFA* being challenged by their own tactics! The only exceptions to this were the World Cup spin-off editions.

Imagery from *FIFA Football 2002* – the players involved are up for debate.

FIFA Football 2003 | Released: October 2002

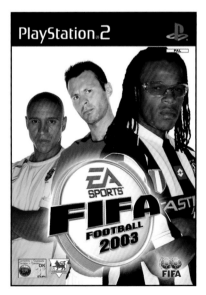

In a throwback to *FIS* – which was lauded for including crowd noise – 2003 included unique chants and songs for 17 of Europe's elite, who also had their own stadia. This was part of the new Club Championship Mode, which was accompanied by an expansion of the TV-style highlights, the package extended to include half-time and full-time clips from the game.

FIFA Football 2003 added 'Freestyle Control', allowing fancy flicks and tricks, for gamers to do their best virtual impression of Brazil playmaker Ronaldinho, a future cover star and flavour of the season.

It was also the first game in the series to have EA Trax, the official name for the in-game playlist, which included songs by Avril Lavigne, Fatboy Slim and Ms Dynamite, as part of the agreement secured by EA across their sports games.

After five years of licensing single songs to be the official *FIFA* 'tracks', *FIFA Football 2003* was a significant step towards establishing the Spotify-esque model of in-game music streaming.

Marc Aubanel said: "We were licensing music ad hoc in each dev team at that point of time. Eventually, a guy called Steve Schnur started to organise this rag-tag music licensing process, which was costing a lot of money.

"So then we had one voice going to the band and licensing three games, rather than having three teams going to that same band. He really brought it together.

"At that time, Napster had died, the industry was suffering, CD sales had started to drop, people had started downloading, so musicians were looking for additional revenue sources. That really was the early streaming distribution of music, ahead of Spotify, etc."

**Ryan Giggs' appearance in *FIFA Football 2003*
was quite a leap forward.**

FIFA 2003 didn't just sound good, it looked good, too. EA Sports reworked the outdated 'DirectX 7' graphics used in its two predecessors, allowing visible improvements in the appearance of kits, stadiums and players - with a big increase in level of detail.

FIFA Football 2004 | **Released: October 2003**

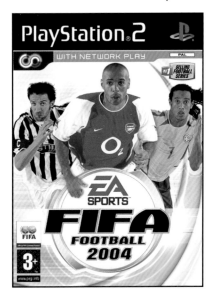

Lower league and Latino fans rejoice – *FIFA Football 2004* saw secondary divisions and teams from Latin America (other than Brazil) added to the series for the first time.

The headline addition from EA Sports' perspective, though, was the online mode, while new gameplay feature Off The Ball was added, allowing for control of a secondary player.

EA Trax continued to grow, *FIFA Football 2004* boasted 28 songs, including stellar names such as Goldfrapp, The Jam, Kasabian, Kings of Leon, Radiohead and The Stone Roses.

Main cover star, Thierry Henry, was to abandon the *FIFA* brand, though – instead signing for rivals Konami, where he fronted *Pro Evolution Soccer 5* with Chelsea defender John Terry. At the time, it was probably representative of the contrasting fortunes of the two games, though EA missing out was to prove the exception rather than the rule.

David Beckham in *FIFA Football 2004*.

FIFA Football 2005 | Released: October 2004

The increasing threat of *Pro Evolution Soccer* forced EA's hand, bringing forward the 2005 release to early October 2004 – though that was also influenced by the early 2005 release of *FIFA Street*, a first in that series. The battle with Konami, though, was becoming a major one, with critics at the time generally leaning towards *PES*. As ever, those at EA weren't going to take this rivalry lying down – and, having lost Arsenal talisman Henry to *PES*, they simply signed up his club captain, Patrick Vieira, to front *FIFA Football 2005*.

Alongside him were two European super-strikers who would go on to flop in the UK – Andriy Shevchenko, who scored the winning penalty for Milan in the 2003 Champions League final, and Fernando Morientes, who was the tournament's top scorer in the following campaign, for Monaco.

FIFA 06 | Released: October 2005

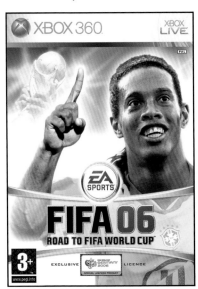

With *PES* in their sights, EA Sports completely overhauled the game engine, rewriting more than half of the game's code and discarding features such as Off The Ball.

Similarly dramatic improvements were made to Career Mode, which now offered a 15-year lifespan, and two features that would become part of Ultimate Team – team chemistry, and in-app purchases, the latter to unlock higher-rated teams.

In the game's retro section was a playable version of *FIFA International Soccer*, though it was titled '*FIFA 94*', while online was another focus, with the *FIFA 06* Lounge offering a whole host of different ways to play over the internet.

A Classic XI team also made its *FIFA* debut, their home kit the same as the one worn by the Allies in cult football film *Escape To Victory*, with the away kit inspired by Sylvester Stallone's goalkeeper jersey. They, along with the World XI, used Cardiff's Millennium Stadium as their home ground, with the two teams unlockable through *FIFA* Points, another soon-to-be-common element of the series.

FIFA 07 | **Released: September 2006**

A game that lacked a killer feature, or groundbreaking introduction, but which continued *FIFA*'s growth, with more than 500 teams, in 27 leagues, using over 10,000 licensed players. The rights to virtually the entire football world belonged to EA Sports.

The addition of Interactive Leagues saw players track real world fixtures each week, from the Premier League, Bundesliga, Ligue 1 and the Mexican League, representing the team they supported. This was to prove popular and has remained in the series, in one way or another, ever since. Another future mainstay to arrive in *FIFA 07* was the finesse button's introduction, offering players more of a placed shot.

This was the first *FIFA* game to sponsor a football team – backing Accrington Stanley during the 2007/08 campaign.

**Ronaldo with another piece of trickery in *FIFA 07*
– soon, EA would be doing the same.**

FIFA 08 | Released: September 2007

Another milestone release for the *FIFA* franchise, this was the first in the series to be released on the new PlayStation 3, with critics suitably impressed by the game's transition to the new generation of consoles.

Rik Henderson explained: "The first FIFA to be released on the PS3 was a major breakthrough. After going toe-to-toe for so long, this was, at last, a FIFA game that was unarguably better than PES and anything else on the market.

"That was so important. Since then, the gap between the two games has just grown and grown to the extent that FIFA no longer really has a rival."

Part of that appeal came down to the new Be A Pro mode – where gamers play as one individual outfield player – and co-operative online play. A control tweak was introduced in the form of using the right analog stick to switch players while defending.

Embracing a new platform wasn't the only reason *FIFA 08* earned plaudits, with Senior Gameplay Producer Aaron McHardy hailing a pivotal moment – and the most decisive in recent history – in the series. He says: "The sophistication of our engine has built up over the last decade, and a big part of that has been our kicking error system, which was first implemented into FIFA 08.

"It has blossomed into a bunch of other things. It started as just a way to develop good resulting trajectories in kicking – so, when you kick the ball, we understand all of the context of what's going on around you, when you strike the ball, to give you an appropriate outcome that isn't random, we hate random on gameplay. We try to get to the nuts and bolts of everything that happens.

"But that system looked at every context when you strike the ball – if the ball's bouncing, if it's rolling in laterally, if it's coming in fast towards you, if it's got spin on it, if it's wet. All of these things factor in to try and mathematically work out the likelihood you miskick the ball and, if

Ah, Fernando Torres, back when he was good – representing Liverpool in *FIFA 08*.

you do, how's it going to react, based on all those contexts. So that started on FIFA 08 and we've been building on it ever since.

"In FIFA 09, it grew, and we put in a tool we have on the dev team, called The Testing Game – known as TG – which is a file we throw around for testing purposes as a fast way to iterate on the game. Building on the kicking error system with TG allowed us to set up a scenario to play repeatedly to see the outcome, which allowed us to iterate and tune and change things so that we got believable outcomes all the time.

"Then that grew into this greater thing over the years which is called Juego Fantastico now, which takes the concept of having bite-sized pieces of a game to make it perfect and applying them across the entire game. So, now you can do it as a player is controlling the ball or to see how someone reacts emotionally to being slide-tackled. It's ballooned into this tool we use across the game.

"It allows our game to be emergent and sophisticated and realistic. That's why it's been the most impactful innovation of the last ten years. Juego Fantastico is now the underlying technology we use to build Skill Games."

Becks of the net: then-LA Galaxy star David Beckham in 'pivotal release' *FIFA 08*.

Wayne Rooney through the FIFA years: how the image-conscious England captain has appeared throughout the FIFA series…

A young looking Rooney in *FIFA 07*.

Rooney's facial features are more detailed in *FIFA 08*.

Wahey-ne! Rooney's realism is remarkable in *FIFA 09*

Motion captured – Rooney is a picture of realism these days. Above, in *FIFA 12*.

FIFA 09 | **Released: October 2008**

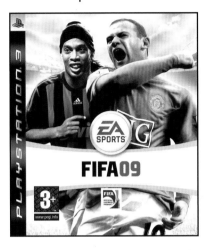

An otherwise relatively nondescript release, with few stand-out changes – more updates to existing features – *FIFA 09* actually reimagined the series more than many others, as it introduced Ultimate Team as a downloadable add-on in March 2009, the impact of which we explore in Chapter Nine.

Other attention grabbing additions included the new Adidas Live Season feature, which was actually supposed to be the game mode that normalised micro-transactions – including one free league until the end of the 2009 season, further divisions could be added for £4.99 – and user-controlled celebrations, which was perhaps surprisingly popular, given its minor impact on the overall game.

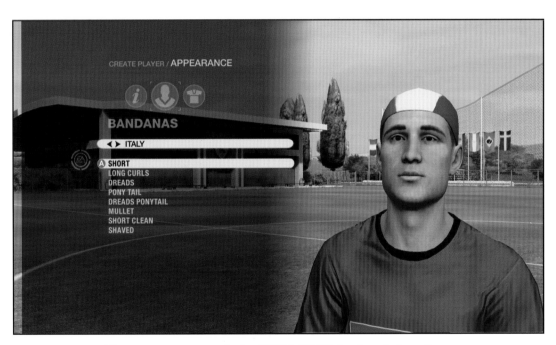

Player creator mode in *FIFA 09*. This chap's bandana was far too continental for us.

A tweak to the physics came with an improved collision system, allowing for more realistic results when two players clashed – rather than rogue limbs going straight through opponents. Painful!

FIFA 10 | **Released: October 2009**

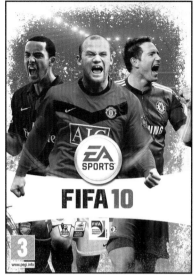

The arrival of EA Sports' Game Face system – where users can scan their head to create an in-game face to put onto a player – demonstrated the technological advances made in the series. It was added to *FIFA* after proving successful in stable-mates such as *Madden*. That an NFL game was playing guinea pig to a soccer title was surely an impossibility 20 years earlier.

But, now, the roles had reversed for the two flagship titles. As Marc Aubanel recalls: "The first year FIFA surpassed Madden in sales... clearly, that's when we knew we had a massive success. Madden had been out for a while before FIFA. It was established, and Americans are football crazy. So, to surpass that was a big milestone for a soccer game.

"Madden was stuck in America, whereas FIFA was constantly moving into new markets – North Korea, China, and Brazil. That's when it became the priority at EA."

Improvements came in handy for the new Virtual Pro mode, where players create a footballer and take him through four Be A Pro seasons; he can also be used in the Manager Mode and in online matches.

For Aaron McHardy, this was the iteration that took the series away from typical video games: "There have been a lot of significant milestones along the way that have changed the game. The first one that comes to mind, as an obvious big shift, was when we added 360 dribbling in FIFA 10, which took us away from classic video games where there are eight directions. It added a whole new dimension to the game."

The game's tagline – "How big can football get" – served as an

An action shot from *FIFA 10* of Lord Bendtner, himself, celebrating a goal. Naturally.

accurate insight into the thinking at EA Sports at the time, as the series was about to take-off in terms of depth and quality.

This Rooney, from *FIFA 10*, is good, but does look a little like a Halloween mask.

FIFA 11 | **Released: October 2010**

Though the cover stars were Kaka and Wayne Rooney, it would almost have been more appropriate for *FIFA 11* to have Gigi Buffon, Petr Cech or one of their contemporaries on the case, as it was the first to allow gamers to play as a goalkeeper. The Be A Goalkeeper mode meant that 11 vs 11 online matches were possible for the first time.

A new passing system, known as Pro Passing, was introduced, offering increased directional intuition, allowing for more accuracy, while the popular Manager Mode was scrapped, and replaced with Career Mode, which included a new option to play as player-manager.

Another new addition – tested in a World Cup game first, like Ultimate Team – was the introduction of the 'Two Button' control system, a simplified version of the game's, at times, complex commands.

The Creation Centre was added online where users could come up with custom material – such as teams, kits and players – and download them into their games, or share with friends.

Be A Pro mode from *FIFA 11* – with a tester who is, clearly, reluctant to track back.

The PC version of *FIFA 11* used the same game engine as the PlayStation 3 and Xbox 360 versions, while it was the last time a game in the series would appear on Nintendo's handheld DS system. On the Wii, slightly surprisingly, street football returned – harking back to the earliest days of the series – in the form of a five-on-five mode.

The soundtrack included established bands like Linkin Park, Scissor Sisters, Massive Attack, Gorillaz, plus up and comers such as Two Door Cinema Club.

FIFA 12 | **Released: September 2011**

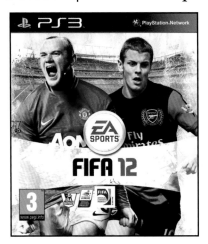

Described as a 'revolutionary year' in the *FIFA* series, by line producer David Rutter, with huge changes to gameplay, including the all-new Player Impact Engine, introduced after years of development. It reimagined the physics of *FIFA*, taking the game to all new levels of realism, with advanced animation creating authentic-looking collisions.

Also new to *FIFA 12* was the Tactical Defending system, giving real emphasis on the backline for the first time, placing more control in the hands of the gamer when going backwards, as well as forwards. Rather than delegate defensive responsibility to the AI by holding down the 'press' button, the process was made far more manual.

Similarly, intuitive tweaks were made to dribbling, with Precision Dribbling allowing for closer control, and AI – now known as Pro Player Intelligence – enabling computer players to react according to circumstance, rather than preset instructions. So a winger would only cross if their teammate in the penalty area was good in the air, otherwise seeking to cut back inside and change the angle of attack.

New mode Head to Head Seasons reflected the increasing online focus, with gamers ranked on their performance against other players around the world, rather than versus the computer.

UEFA Euro 2012 was released as a downloadable expansion pack rather than boxed copy, as the digital world was fully embraced by EA Sports, inspired, no doubt, by the success of Ultimate Team, which was by now part of the full *FIFA* game on disc.

Interestingly, EA tried to spread *FIFA 12* as far and wide as possible, clearly happy with the work they had done. It boasted a Nintendo 3DS version, with all modes bar online gaming; it was a launch title for the PS Vita; had editions for the iPhone, iPad and iPod Touch; and became the first official port to Mac in the series.

With handsome saves such as this screenshot from *FIFA 12*,
is it any wonder Joe Hart is an advert star?

FIFA 13 | **Released: September 2012**

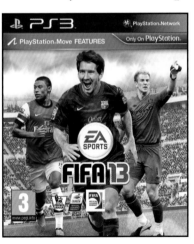

An evolutionary year on the revolutionary/evolutionary cycle, adding to the work done by its immediate predecessor. Attacking Intelligence made virtual players more savvy – they were now able to analyse space independently.

Complete Dribbling was the next stage of Precision Dribbling, allowing full 360-degree movement of touches and a whole host of new options for players while on the attack.

Similarly dangerous was the new First Touch Control, which, effectively, removed the automatic 'perfect' first-touch and opened up the game to defensive lapses and clumsy losses of possession, just as in real life.

This was the first *FIFA* to be compatible with the Xbox Kinect and PlayStation Move – the movement controlled fads of the time – though it failed to really become a huge part of the game. This was despite a smart innovation in career mode where you could get sacked for swearing at the ref if your Kinect picked it up.

Moments like this make the celebrations options genius.
Mario Balotelli savours a goal in *FIFA 13*.

FIFA 14 | **Released: September 2013**

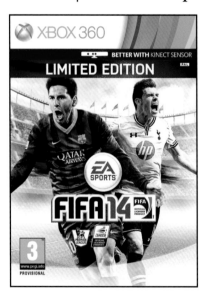

The first release on the current generation of games consoles, *FIFA* was amongst the first games to arrive on the Xbox One and PlayStation 4 and seen as a key pawn in the battle between the two; Microsoft securing exclusive Ultimate Team content to tempt gamers away from their rival, Sony.

Given the advanced graphical power available to them, EA Sports' unveiling of a new game engine – the Ignite Engine – was probably to be expected, with particular improvements in the match day environment, the weather and the noticeably realistic crowd.

As with the previous two iterations, gameplay improvements focused on realistic movement – with True Player Motion – and advanced AI that gives players human emotions, such as anxiety during key moments of a match.

Another breakthrough came in North America, where, for the first time, the game wasn't referred to as '*FIFA* Soccer' but released simply as *FIFA 14* in the territory, with a Javier Hernandez-fronted cover, in addition to the global version starring Lionel Messi.

And broadcast-worthy matchday presentations emerged as a focus, much to the relief of

Producer Santiago Jaramillo: "When we moved to the next gen, broadcast was one of the things where FIFA was lagging behind. It was that kind of immersion that was lacking, it looked very generically branded – it needed a lot of love. It's definitely come on in leaps and bounds on next gen, after not really being the focus of investment for many years."

FIFA 15 | **Released: September 2014**

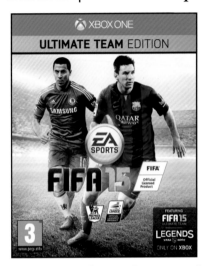

The first in the series to be fully licensed by the Premier League, after securing a deal to be the division's Official Sports Technology Partner, allowing inclusion of all 20 stadiums and the league's player pool head-scanned for better likeness. Similarly, Serie A was fully licensed.

Lifelike additions extended to other visual elements, including the official Premier League scoreboards, true-to-life advertising hoardings, actual referees, and real-world supporter chants.

Ultimate Team was again the recipient of focus, with two new features introduced – the addition of loan signings of players, and the Concept Squad, where players can put together an ideal line-up to aim for.

For Rik Henderson, it was a serious step in the right direction: "*FIFA 15* was a huge breakthrough for the series, huge. The amount of detail they put into it. For the first time in its entire history the players actually looked like players, they didn't look like sort of chunky people playing football, but human beings. What sells games is including a lot of new features around the existing *FIFA* experience, and it had a lot of that."

FIFA 15 also saw a renewed focus on goalkeepers – who have long been something of an engima within football, let alone virtual recreations. For Aaron McHardy, it's been a focus that has demanded a lot of hard work from his team of gameplay developers.

"In older games, we realised we had a problem with the goalkeeper, and the cost to maintain the goalkeeper because it had a whole suite of animations that were separate from everyone else on the pitch. To maintain this database of all the different kind of saves he could do was tough, and immensely expensive.

"So we had to find a technologically advanced way to use our animations to solve that problem. We went to the drawing board and developed this for a couple of years, up until we put it in FIFA 15, and for FIFA 16 we've doubled down on the efforts, just to try and make sure that it's balanced and sound.

"That whole world of the goalkeeper is enough to keep one person completely consumed for an entire year: trying to understand the ins and outs of how every single save is made, and the decisions that are being made to be able to get to the ball, the amount of calculations that go into that on the AI and animation sides. It's mindnumbing.

"There's a group of probably four or five guys who have done nothing else but dedicate themselves to understanding that system, how it works and their behaviours. Like understanding the thought process that goes on in a goalkeeper's head, when he's going to 'cheat' to one side or another of his goal before a shot. And then implementing a detail like that into our code – which can be all encompassing.

The high definition gameplay of *FIFA 15* is worlds away from the start of the series.

Likewise, original Lead Programmer Jan Tian is impressed with how the game he once worked on has developed. He says: "Today, the style is still there, but it has much better graphics, much better sound, the logic is much more complicated because you have so much computer power to use, your joypad control is 360-degree, you have the finite power control for passing and shooting.

"I'm really proud that I paved the foundation for the kind of gameplay we see today, the so-called auto-assist, a term which was almost copyrighted. Before then, you would dribble the ball from one end to the other and score. There was no team-play, no AI, no opponent logic to talk about. Back then, the computer power was so slow. You had an eight directional joypad, which is not good enough for passing. Now, it's incredible."

Smash-hit: Clint Dempsey, shown here in *FIFA 15*, reflects the soaring popularity of football, and *FIFA*, in the US.

FIFA's progress is undeniable but, for a certain period of time, in the mid-2000s, if you had to guess which football title would be receiving such praise and accolades a decade on, the most common answer would *not* be *FIFA*…

How FIFA fared in other guises

For many gamers, the main *FIFA* series has been the only one they know, although EA Sports have been sure to explore different avenues for their prized franchise: the popular but monopolised management game market, for example, with *FIFA Manager*.

They have also continued their fondness for licenses with World Cup, European Championships, and Champions League-specific spin-offs. In turn, with *FIFA Street*, they produced an entirely different type of football video game – continuing to innovate whilst they dominated.

And actually, although these titles have never managed to replicate the success of the *FIFA* series 'proper', they have often proved a valuable proving ground for key features, gameplay elements and staff acquisitions. Besides which, some pretty decent spin-off games have emerged in their own right, too.

FIFA Street | Released: 2005

Inspired by the success of other 'Street' releases across EA Sports' catalogue, this was a more arcade-y version of *FIFA*, focussing on trickery rather than tactics – with European Footballer of the Year Ronaldinho the obvious, and natural, poster boy.

Intended to give a feel for the impromptu kick-abouts that are common – in popular mythology, anyway – on the beaches of Brazil and back-streets of Britain, the game felt like *FIFA* had cut loose somewhat.

For freelance games reviewer Jamie Nightingale, it was a clear appeal to a new demographic: "By shifting the gameplay style to something fresh and exciting, FIFA Street really caught the attention of the younger gamers. After all, it is this group of people who are most likely to desire more playing freedom – older gamers get swept up in tactics and stats.

"FIFA Street made it easier to pick up and play, with the most rookie of players able to play like a stylish pro. In many ways, it was a gateway into the full FIFA game for first time players.

"The first release, despite initial scepticism – and mixed critical reviews – was a success, in that it at least proved the idea valuable enough to continue with a successor.

"For many, this looked like it was going to be the future of the series – after all, everything EA did turned to gold usually. In this case, looking back, maybe they had to make do with silver."

The four-on-four games focussed more on great tricks than goals, with respect being the most valuable currency; it was used to build up a team of recognised players, including Ronaldinho and Cristiano Ronaldo, as the gamer progressed through various street pitches around the world.

Rapper MC Harvey, of So Solid Crew, was the brilliantly bizarre choice of commentator.

Cristiano Ronaldo performs a trick in the original *FIFA Street*.

FIFA Street 2 | Released: 2006

The second game in the series saw a transfer on the front cover, as then Manchester United sensation Cristiano Ronaldo replaced Ronaldinho – EA perhaps foreseeing the slump in the Brazilian's career that was to come not much later.

It introduced a new 'trick stick beat' system and an array of new tricks. With the first game in the series delivering a concept, it was *FIFA Street 2* that provided more of a tangible sense of game – with dramatic improvements on its successor.

Rule The Streets was akin to the Pro Player mode in normal *FIFA*, with gamers taking on the role of an individual player, and using points to buy clothing and improve his rating.

Amongst the unlockable opponents in the game were a selection of Legends – something that would later be replicated in Ultimate Team – including England's very own street star, Paul Gascoigne.

Also notable about the game was that it had its own in-game radio station, presented by Zane Lowe from Radio 1 – music, again, a key element of the *FIFA* series.

In terms of critical reception, *FIFA Street 2* got similar marks to the first in the series, but faced more scrutiny than the original – which seemed to ride on its novelty factor – with many negative reviews pointing to shaky defending as an issue. Which seems harsh in a game that centres around tricky attackers and skills...

Action from *FIFA Street 2*, which improved dramatically on its predecessor.

FIFA Street 3 | **Released: 2008**

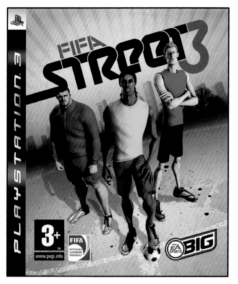

Is this the only time Peter Crouch has been a poster boy for something other than very tall men and questionable dance skills?

Hard though it may be to believe, the gangly England striker was chosen to displace Ronaldo on the cover of *FIFA Street 3* – along with returning star Ronaldinho, and a not particularly flattering interpretation of Italian midfielder Gennaro Gattuso.

But that was part of *FIFA Street's* charm – the cartoon-like characters, more fitting with the likes of stablemate *SSX* than hyper-realistic *FIFA*, matched the arcade feel of the gameplay.

This was the last title developed by EA Sports BIG, the studio set up to explore extreme sports and the arcade equivalents of mainstream sports, before its dissolution in 2008. The experiment with a new gaming stable led to the conclusion that EA Sports was franchise-heavy enough.

Peter Crouch wins a header – while a scary looking Wayne Rooney watches on.

Which is a shame, as the *FIFA Street* series appeared to have found its feet in its third release – which included more than 250 players from 18 different international outfits, each appearing in a caricature style, boasting their own hero qualities.

Again, critical reviews were mixed, but this was another stride forward for the series – it was the most tactically aware release of *FIFA Street*, with players now falling into different categories, an acknowledgement that not every player has to be a freestyle footballer of sorts.

Alongside these types, known as Tricksters, there were also Enforcers, Playmakers and Finishers, to give a new dimension to gameplay. Environments, too, had become ambitious and alive, and the whole *FIFA Street 3* experience was an enjoyable one.

FIFA Street | Released: 2012

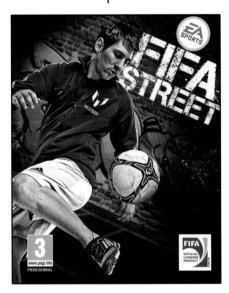

Though this wasn't styled as a 'fourth instalment' of the same series – due to development for the game moving in-house at EA Sports from BIG, as discussed above – this was the next part, presumably dusted off as an opportunity to make the most of signing Lionel Messi to the *FIFA* brand.

The creative director for this game was Gary Paterson – the gameplay genius credited with resurrecting the main *FIFA* series, and clearly hoping to repeat the trick. And, unlike its predecessors, *FIFA Street 4* was more involved with the main series, using elements of the *FIFA 12* engine for this reboot.

The other big change was that the caricatured characters were replaced by more *FIFA* style graphics, with a more realistic look adopted. The main nucleus of the game, though, remained the same – small-sided matches in street venues. Skills were the order of the day, boasting double the number of skill moves offered in *FIFA 12*, and fifty more than *FIFA Street 3*.

Gameplay innovations such as Street Ball Control, and a new 'ATTACK' dribbling system, bolstered the experience, while huge depth was offered, with players from 3,000 different teams available in the game – the first in the series to add club sides as well as nations.

In a scathing reflection on its predecessor, line producer Sid Misra, talking at the unveiling of the game to *GameSpot*, said: "What we really wanted to do is come out with the first truly great street football experience. There hasn't been one yet – FIFA Street 1, 2 and 3 barely tried."

The game boasted 36 different venues, a 24-song soundtrack, and hugely improved reviews – up around 15% on previous titles in the series – but hasn't been followed up on. Yet…

FIFA Manager

The longest running – and therefore, presumably, most successful – spin-off to the main *FIFA* series, EA Sports' perseverance with management games eventually paid off.

The first football management game released by EA Sports was in 1997 – when *FIFA* was just five iterations old – as the company looked to take on PC giant *Football Manager* (formerly known as *Championship Manager*). That battle has been a struggle, with the name of EA's management game changing several times.

That first release included the late Sir Bobby Robson on the cover, was titled *FIFA Soccer Manager*, and was best known for its complete stadium builder. Using 300 different elements, users could create a venue of up to 300,000 seats.

The next year's title was entirely reimagined. A new license was secured and the game was given the catchy title of *The F.A. Premier League Football Manager 99*. Sadly, this version was best known for its bugs – such as Manchester United getting relegated in the first season – but the series name, incredibly, stuck around for four iterations.

For the 2002 reboot, again fronted by Robson, the game was reimagined as *Total Club Manager 2003*, with the Premier League logo prominent in the bottom right-hand corner of the cover.

It was this brand that started to build some recognition. Jose Mourinho starred on the cover for the third iteration, *Total Club Manager 2005*, after being appointed as manager of Chelsea, following worldwide fame with his Champions League success at Porto. On the German version, meanwhile, was Felix Magath. A rather different character.

Despite that tie-up, and various other attempts at appealing to the *FIFA* demographic – including the introduction of 'Football Fusion', which allowed owners of both *FIFA 2004* and *TCM 2004* to play matches across the two games – EA would abandon their pursuit of a console-based management game, re-rebooting the series as 'PC only' a year later.

There, it became *FIFA Manager 06* and, like rival *Football Manager*, didn't include a cover star – instead showing the back of a football manager in action. That first title was the only *FIFA Manager* game to include a soundtrack with music from real bands. Stereophonics were the most high-profile contributors to the nine songs licensed.

In theory, the game should have outdone its rival – now made by SEGA – as *FIFA* could boast the graphics and gameplay engine from its main series of games, whereas *Football Manager's* 3D 'highlights' were of nondescript players from a distance.

But, for whatever reason, *FIFA Manager* failed to crack the market and, after nine releases, EA finally decided to give up on management games entirely, retiring from the genre.

For Jamie Nightingale, this was because EA's attention to detail didn't extend to every facet of *FIFA Manager*: "Football management game fans expect detailed minutia of data on everyone and everything in the football world. So, while FIFA Manager was always ahead of the curve when it came to graphics, it lacked that requisite detail to retain players to the series."

FIFA *Manager* had everything going for it but sales.
Which proved a decisive issue.

How EA's soccer series has become dominant in numbers

We'll never know exactly who first piped up and bravely touted football as a sport that EA Sports should invest in – citing, no doubt, its huge global presence in virtually every country outside of America and Canada – but they must now boast a rather large amount of credit in the bank with their employers.

As the sport has generally exploded around the planet, starting with the 1994 US World Cup that followed the release of *FIFA International Soccer*, so too has the market for the *FIFA* series – assisted, too, by the huge increase in gaming and the near ubiquity of consoles amid home entertainment systems.

By the end of 2010, the *FIFA* games had sold more than 100million copies worldwide, with *FIFA 13* setting the record for the fastest selling sports game ever – shifting 4.5million copies in the first week of release, generating £120million in revenue.

In the UK, it became just the second franchise to sell more than a million units within a day, and it was the number one selling game in 43 countries the week it launched. A success, it's fair to say.

Those incredible sales figures were soon prompting further record breaking activity, as three days after *FIFA 13* launched worldwide, EA recorded the busiest day for online gaming for a single title in its history, with 810,000 people playing the game simultaneously. In all, the game sold 8.15million copies – the best-selling sports game in history.

That success should have been expected, given the popularity of the game's demo – which was downloaded 4.6million times on Xbox and PlayStation 3, with more than a million pre-orders. Online, the game trended globally on Twitter – with 287,000 social mentions, 97% of which were tweets. The majority of those, intriguingly, were from the US, with 153,000 tweets.

It seems that, despite the initial disinterest in the title, America has become a hotbed of *FIFA* fans – okay, so maybe a 'warm' bed, but it is certainly making a mark: the States is behind only the UK as the second best-selling country for the game.

More than a third of American *FIFA* players, 34% to be precise, become pro soccer fans after playing the video game. That means they actually start following a team, and tracking the real world goings-on.

And, increasingly, the teams selected are from the MLS – with a 112% increase recorded between *FIFA 14* and *FIFA 15* in terms of people playing with a team from the division, Seattle Sounders proving the most popular.

If it can conquer a sceptical America then, clearly, it can rule globally. And that's exactly what's happened. Since the first release in 1993, the series has produced close to £4billion in revenue – which makes it, by some distance, EA's biggest selling franchise.

That demand is reflected in the localisation process the game goes through for its millions of players. Since 2011, the game has been localised into 18 languages and been made available in 51 different countries.

Even museums are paying an interest in the *FIFA* series – with the National Football Museum in Manchester running their *Pitch to Pixel: The World of Football Gaming* exhibition from October 23rd, 2015.

In it, the museum will explore the evolution of football video games generally, from the first home computer titles to the immersive world of *FIFA*, featuring plenty of historic football titles to play on.

And the *FIFA* interest bandwagon doesn't stop there. There's even a book about the series! What do you mean you hadn't noticed? You're reading it now…

Bournemouth defender, and avid *FIFA* player, Steve Cook is interviewed by the National Football Museum for *Pitch to Pixel*.

FIFA Records

Some of the most impressive – and seemingly impossible – records achieved by *FIFA* gamers from around the world, certified by the *Guinness World Records Gamer's Edition 2016*.

Greatest margin of victory against the computer

On *FIFA World Cup 2014*, this remarkable record is 321 goals, achieved by German gamer Patrick Hadler, while playing as his native country against the Cook Islands. Patrick also set the record for *FIFA 13*, with a 307-goal margin, and *FIFA 14*, with 322 goals. We could all learn a thing or two from the teaching assistant.

Highest earning *FIFA* Gamer

In 2013, Swedish gamer Ivan "BorasLegend" Lapanje banked $140,000 for winning the *Virgin Gaming EA Sports FIFA Challenge 2013* in Las Vegas. Nicely done, sir.

Longest *FIFA* marathon

Christopher Cook, we salute you. The Londoner/legend spent an incredible 48 hours 49 minutes and 41 seconds playing *FIFA 15* to raise money for the charity Special Effect – which supports disabled gamers. Even though Chris lost the feeling in his hands, he's a true champion, rallying to win his final two matches, before heading straight to bed, no doubt.

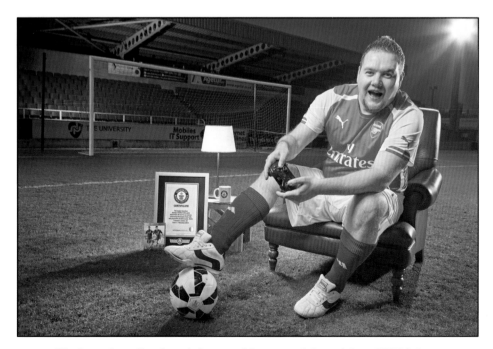

Christopher Cook celebrates his record-breaking *FIFA* feat.

The ultimate crossbar challenge

This is a quite ridiculous record – for the most consecutive crossbar hits in one minute. It was achieved first by American gamer Shawn Alvarez, before being matched by Italian Edoardo Lo Baido a month later, both hitting the woodwork four times in a row. Which is some going. Or, as we call it at my club, typical.

Best *FIFA* juggler

Another trickster record, this time claimed by Australia-based Brit Aaron Softley. He snared the most consecutive juggles in one minute, with 166. That's approximately 16 times my record.

Deadliest penalty taker

Finally, an Englishman who can be trusted from the spot. Christopher 'Jeeby' Hull, from Liverpool, scored 26 consecutive penalty kicks on *FIFA 10*. Have England even scored that many in the whole of history?

Most prolific soccer video game commentator

It is, of course, the one and only John Motson – who commentated on the *FIFA* series between *FIFA 97* and *FIFA Football 2005*, a spell of eight years and nine titles. Clive Tyldesley and Martin Tyler have been the subsequent voices of the English versions.

Most prolific *FIFA* cover star

This title belongs to Wayne Rooney – for whom it might feel like catching the bouquet at the wedding of your ex. The England captain appeared on seven successive *FIFA* covers, starting with *FIFA 06*. A pretty impressive run that demonstrates his enduring appeal – even if he was replaced for *FIFA 13*.

FIFA's favourite platform

Was, evidently, the PlayStation 2. EA released more games on the second-generation of Sony's flagship games console than any other: 19 PS2 titles. That started with *FIFA Football 2001*, and continued with releases every year for 13 years, ending with *FIFA 14*.

Most popular *FIFA* iteration

No title in the *FIFA* series has sold as many copies as *FIFA 14* (yet), which shifted more than 14.5million units globally. Beat that, *FIFA 16*.

In *FIFA 2015*, the series boasted incredible breadth and depth, featuring 35 licensed leagues, over 600 clubs and more than 16,000 players. Its very own footballing universe. Amongst the leagues featured are the South Korean K League Classic, Norway's Tippeligaen, Mexico's LIGA Bancomer and Chile's Campeonato Nacional.

For *FIFA 16*, the most publicised new playable teams in the game are the 12 women's national sides, with gamers now able to take control of the female line-ups from Australia, Brazil, Canada, China, England, France, Germany, Italy, Mexico, Spain, Sweden and the USA.

Nine new officially licensed stadiums have been added to *FIFA 16,* taking the total tally to 50 – including newly promoted English Premier League sides Watford (Vicarage Road), Norwich (Carrow Road) and Bournemouth (The Vitality Stadium).

Norwich's Carrow Road gets the *FIFA* treatment.

The other English stadium added is League Two outfit Portsmouth's Fratton Park, by way of tribute to late Creative Director Simon Humber – dubbed 'the Daddy of Ultimate Team' – who passed away in the buildup to the game. The stadium includes a wreath of flowers in one of the goals, as testament to the lifelong Pompey fan, mirroring the real-life tribute paid to him by the club's supporters in May 2015.

Existing British stadiums in the game include the entire Premier League, while relegated sides QPR, Hull City and Burnley all continue to feature, alongside the English national stadium, Wembley, the only international venue included.

Further new stadiums added to *FIFA 16* include Marseille's Stade Velodrome, joining league rivals PSG and Lyon; and Borussia Park, home to Borussia Monchengladbach, following their Champions League qualification for the 2015/16 season.

Marseille's Stade Velodrome offers an impressive roof to capture in-game.

The other Bundesliga venues in the game include the Allianz Arena – the home of Bayern and 1860 Munich – as well as the stadiums for Hamburg, Hertha Berlin, Borussia Dortmund and Schalke.

Bournemouth's Dean Court ground is done justice by EA Sports' art team.

King Abdullah Sports City, which plays hosts to Al-Ittihad & Al-Ahli in Saudi Arabia, joins the King Fahd International Stadium, where Al Hilal, Al Nassr and Al Shabab all play their football.

In South America, River Plate's El Monumental follows La Bombonera, the iconic home of fierce rivals Boca Juniors; while Seattle Sounders' CenturyLink Field is the latest MLS arena to be added, joining the Vancouver Whitecaps.

The other clubs to have officially licensed stadiums in the game are Barcelona, Real Madrid, Atletico Madrid and Valencia from La Liga; Serie A's Juventus Stadium (Juventus), San Siro (AC Milan and Inter), and Stadio Olimpico (Lazio and Roma); Mexico's Club America, Dutch giants Ajax, and Ukrainian outfit Shakhtar Donetsk. That makes fifty licensed stadiums in all.

Take a virtual pew at Watford's Vicarage Road on *FIFA 16*.

*

Here's a stat for the modern age – measuring and illustrating something's popularity against Facebook. Very 2015, I know. But it is telling that *FIFA* fans spend more time playing the game, at an average of 57 minutes per day, than the typical person spends on Mark Zuckerberg's social network, which amounts to 46 minutes.

Further testament to that virtual-social theme is the soaring popularity of Ultimate Team – already *FIFA*'s most successful mode, and a runaway success – which records some astonishing statistics.

In the first five years of the new mode – two of which were spent as optional downloads, so not even on the *FIFA* disc – there were 21.8million unique FUT players. In *FIFA 14* alone, there were 725million Ultimate Team matches played – equating to 264,000 per day, or 11,000 an hour – and almost 1.5billion transfers listed, as the swapaholic gamers got stuck in.

That was reflective of the all-round success enjoyed by *FIFA 14*. For every 90 minutes of real time – i.e. one real football match, minus breaks and injury time – the game recorded

459,000 matches featuring 3.66million shots, 991,000 goals, 1.9million saves and 338,000 victories. Phew.

Mind blown? Well *FIFA*'s not done yet. In *FIFA 15*, there were 140million matches played between Premier League teams alone, spawning 333million goals. Which is only just short of the real thing. In all, more than 13billion hours of gaming were logged on the game – including over 211million Ultimate Team sessions, and 3.4billion goals scored.

As of April 2015, the *FIFA* series has generated global sales of 146million – outdoing *Madden*, the nearest sports title on the sales list, which has sold 110million copies.

And, perhaps, the stat that matters most – EA's license to use the *FIFA* title runs until 2022. Which guarantees us at least seven more years of the series as we know it.

Heading for another goal – both James Rodriguez and *FIFA 16*.

Most Popular…

…Premier League match-ups on *FIFA 15*

1. Manchester United vs Chelsea, 7.9million fixtures
2. Chelsea vs Manchester City, 7.5million
3. Manchester United vs Manchester City, 5.8million

4. Manchester United vs Arsenal, 5.4million
5. Arsenal vs Chelsea, 4.7million

No prizes for guessing the next fixture in this sequence

...Premier League goalscorers on *FIFA 15*

1. Diego Costa, Chelsea, 56.5million goals
2. Sergio Aguero, Manchester City, 36.7million
3. Eden Hazard, Chelsea, 34.7million
4. Robin van Persie, Manchester United, 27.7million
5. Radamel Falcao, Manchester United, 26.7million

Wayne Rooney must be gutted to have finished below the two strikers he saw off in real life.

**Yes, lads, we're surprised, too, that Tottenham
didn't feature in these lists. *Cough***

…Global match-ups on *FIFA 14*

1. Bayern Munich (40% victory rate) vs Real Madrid (39%), 9.6million fixtures
2. Real Madrid (49%) vs Barcelona (33%), 8.9million
3. Bayern Munich (48%) vs Barcelona (33%), 2.5million
4. Real Madrid (45%) vs Manchester City (36%), 2.3million
5. Dortmund (40%) vs PSG (39%), 2.1million

And, in sixth place, Dagenham versus Exeter. No, only kidding.

…Global goalscorers on *FIFA 14*

1. Cristiano Ronaldo, Real Madrid, 35.2million goals
2. Karim Benzema, Real Madrid, 26.7million
3. Mario Mandzukic, Bayern Munich, 20.2million
4. Lionel Messi, Barcelona, 19.4million
5. Neymar, Barcelona, 17.5million

Another year, another record for CR7. He'll probably be asking for his trophy once he's seen this.

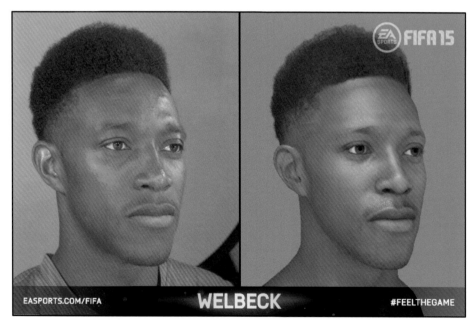

**Welbeck would do well to finish in the top five
Arsenal scorers, let alone global top five.**

...Transferred players on Ultimate Team *FIFA 14*

1. Christian Benteke, Aston Villa
2. Felipe Santana, Schalke
3. Ignazio Abate, AC Milan
4. Luis Gustavo, Wolfsburg
5. Angelo Ogbonna, Juventus
6. Laurent Koscielny, Arsenal
7. Eljero Elia, Wolfsburg
8. Kevin De Bruyne, Chelsea
9. Kieran Gibbs, Arsenal
10. Pepe, Real Madrid

Given the topic of this statistic, it's perhaps not a huge shock that half of the players have been transferred in real life since FIFA 14.

...Most supported club by *FIFA 14* gamers

1. Real Madrid, 717,000 fans
2. Barcelona, 643,000
3. Manchester United, 631,000
4. Arsenal, 598,000
5. Bayern Munich, 381,000

I wonder where EA got the idea for their exclusive club partnership for FIFA 16 with Real Madrid...?

...Day on *FIFA*

Sunday. Apparently. No longer the day of rest, it's now the day of *FIFA* – with more than 232million matches, on average, played every Sunday on *FIFA 15*.

The battle for supremacy with rival Pro Evolution Soccer

With a huge, global presence, *FIFA*'s marketing arm is almost machine-like, as it pumps out region-relevant information, earning publicity everywhere the game goes. Tactics vary, from appealing to the burgeoning female market in North America by putting female players on the *FIFA 16* cover, to arranging pro player tournaments at leading teams in virtually every major European country.

Recognised pretty much universally, the *FIFA* video game is a phenomenon – managing to shrug off even certain PR 'failures' at the organisation from whom EA license the game. Few other companies would be able to do that.

That's testament to EA Sports' forward-thinking commercial department and marketing minds – which was true from the birth of the series, with the actual idea for a soccer title coming from their marketing team.

Chip Lange, who would go on to oversee marketing for that series, reflected: "I was part of the whole decision to create FIFA. I was the product manager on the marketing side, and back then our company was kinda split into two camps. There were the people making the game, and those guys tended to be treated like royalty, they were the rock stars of the industry. Then there were the marketing people, generally people who, once the game was done, stuck it in a pretty box and sold it to Walmart or Game.

"But our little marketing team made some headlines when we started something called EA Sports, which germinated out of the marketing arm of the organisation. All of a sudden, people started seeing that games could be sold, not just because of how great the game was, but because there was a bigger cultural thing going on with EA Sports, and that gave us some credibility.

"This is going to sound crazy, but we made these branded clothing lines, in limited runs, and started wearing them around the country. We made them really hard to get, and all of a sudden the EA Sports thing started taking off right around when we launched FIFA."

If the idea that arguably EA's biggest risk – and subsequent success – came from their marketing team is a bit of a surprise, then the role-model they adopted for the original was less so. Lange explains: "FIFA was, in my opinion, a derivative of our NHL game, which was a runaway phenomenon on the Sega Genesis because of how well the system worked – with crisp passing of the pucks and the one-timer.

"FIFA really tried to leverage that great gameplay and then capitalise on it on a global stage, with a much bigger sport. We had these great engines that were driving the technology on the Genesis back then, and then all of a sudden we had the momentum of this great brand, EA Sports.

"The guys up in Canada – it was a small team – were just obsessed with the sport of soccer. The whole team would go out and play at lunch – they had a field there. From that little corner office of Bruce McMillan's, they created this huge game.

"Bruce was so obsessed with the feel of the product that he would just sit in his office for hours on end, late at night, with the game constantly on. You didn't have all the distractions back then, of the graphics and the opening animation and all that stuff.

"Those games back then were about getting the feel of the buttons right, working with very rudimentary technology to get the players to react in a relatively realistic manner. Because the second they did something that didn't feel right, the fantasy was broken and it was just a game. He worked so hard to get that authenticity in."

As much as the isometric view grabbed gamers' attention, the growing reputation of EA Sports also earned *FIFA* some instant brand recognition – with canny marketing tools making the game a mainstay amongst their key demographic of gamer, according to Lange.

"In the marketing group, we started working on this tagline 'I'm better than you and I can prove it', because we started noticing that the differentiating feature of our games was that people played head-to-head. There was this groundswell in fraternity houses, at colleges, where EA Sports games became a new form of pick-up basketball.

"FIFA was perfect for that; it was such a great multiplayer game in a time before online. Whatever got put in at 2am, when people got back from parties, was the game that became the cultural standard.

"The team was much smaller back then, so we could all get in a room and say, yeah, we want to get as many real teams as we can, we want as many real players, but we want them to play like they do in real life."

Perhaps most famous of the marketing ideas is the now synonymous tagline, read by Andrew Anthony, who revealed that he recorded the line for *nothing* as a favour to an old friend. Speaking in an interview with *GamerHubTV* he said: "It was the early Nineties, and I had a friend in the advertising business, who was approached by EA asking him to do an advert, and he came up with the line.

"It was originally 'If it's in the game – EA Sports, it's in the game' and he called me, up in Toronto, his old buddy, and said 'will you do the voice for this thing, for free?' And I said 'yeah, of course I will. I don't even know what this is, but I've got a free trip down to see you, so, for sure'.

"I recorded it and thought I will never ever hear anything about that again – and 23 years later it has become this mega-brand."

Despite his team's role in supporting the pitch for a soccer series, Chip Lange confirms that it wasn't EA's marketing department that were responsible for Anthony's iconic phrase – read out in that instantly recognisable robotic voice – and says that it became a motivational phrase in-house.

He said: "As simple as it sounds, it really was a unifying design theme that works not only for the marketing campaigns but also for the product. The team realised that the marketing was starting to play a role in the success of the franchises, and the collection of these games under that unifying banner started being greater than the individual whole.

"The challenge we had with FIFA over the years was, in the US you had Madden, NBA and NHL, and then FIFA as a smaller thing. But over in Europe nobody really cared about those other sports, so it was just FIFA. There was this tug and pull between which brand was more powerful – was it FIFA or EA Sports? Should we do a British version of 'EA Sports – it's in the game'? Do they even need the EA Sports brand?"

*

Such marketing ability would prove to be crucial for *FIFA* in their battle with long-term rivals *Pro Evolution Soccer*, made by Japanese developers Konami (having emerged out of the *Goal Storm* series) and previously known as *International Superstar Soccer Pro*.

In fact, though *PES* is now quite some distance behind *FIFA* in terms of both sales figures and actual product, it was the Eastern football game that was dominant for a long time.

For many years, they were top dog – with *FIFA* playing catch-up, in a reverse of the current status the two titles enjoy. For Chip Lange, it was a rivalry that provoked the best from those in Vancouver, working on *FIFA*.

He said: "We were very competitive individuals, we didn't like to lose and PES was a nasty competitor. They were good. Back then they had, in Europe, what Madden enjoyed in the States – it was the common denominator for gaming. If people back then played a soccer video game, Pro Evolution Soccer was usually the thing that got put in the system.

"That was the competitive standard – what the general mass public would use as the benchmark to see who had the best game. PES enjoyed that position for a long time. We were determined to beat them – we'd do focus groups, we'd listen to reviewers, we'd talk to players. It was a hard-fought, long battle.

"Ultimately, a combination of EA being able to consistently evolve our technology year in, year out; continuing to pour endless amounts of resources into the product; and the cool factor of EA Sports, won that battle. Over time, FIFA evolved into being that competitive standard, but it was quite a battle."

The peak of *PES*'s powers probably came in 2004, when they had the audacity to poach *FIFA*'s cover star – and the planet's most marketable player of the time – Thierry Henry. Having fronted *FIFA Football 2004*, the Arsenal striker switched to *Pro Evolution Soccer 4* the following year.

To add insult to injury, he gave a candid interview to accompany the announcement of that decision, which only served to illustrate the dominance of Konami over EA Sports. He said:

"I started off with the Japanese version about ten years ago. I just love Pro Evo – it is by far the closest to real football."

Those quite traumatic comments – the Frenchman had never been quite so passionate about *FIFA* during his time on their payroll – left EA in something of a minor crisis.

That release, *PES 4*, was the first that had included licensed leagues, with Konami following the EA route by signing deals with the top tiers in Italian, Spanish and Dutch football. It also garnered better critic reviews – averaging 93%, generally scoring at least ten points more than *FIFA Football 2005*. *PES 4*, quite incredibly, was the eighth highest critically rated video game of 2004.

For Matt Webster, who was Associate Producer and Designer on early *FIFA* titles, it was a dominance that couldn't be ignored, even within EA's corridors. He said: "We could all see it. In Europe, we were like 'we are in trouble here'.

"I distinctly remember Bruce McMillan coming to visit us in the UK office and opening up to questions, as he hadn't been over for a while. There was a question from the back from a guy called Bob Summerwood, who was a software engineer, and he said 'why isn't FIFA fun anymore?' And you heard the whole room just go 'ooh'. You could hear a pin drop, but he'd done the thing – he'd said what had needed to be said.

"That started an ex-pat invasion, not just of Brits but of Europeans too, to help give that knowledge. Bruce offered Bob a job to go over, and everyone started realising that FIFA had been focusing more on production values and there was no gameplay innovation. It wasn't fun, like Bob had said.

"But, with the new blood brought in, things started to improve. People like Gary Paterson were instrumental in changing it from art-based to gameplay-driven animation, and really kicked it on."

Webster isn't the first, and certainly won't be the last, to highlight Scottish software engineer Paterson's importance – a man often referred to as the title's 'gameplay genius'. He was initially hired in August 2004, recruited from Codemasters after his work on *LMA Manager*, to further the *FIFA Manager* spin-off series, but he was soon switched to the main title, where he made significant changes.

Looking back, the modest Paterson – who would go on to become Creative Director on *FIFA*, and now holds the same position at the Criterion division of the company – is very matter of fact about his impact. He says: "After FIFA Manager 06, I was offered the role of Lead Designer on FIFA 07 on the PlayStation 2. Me and a guy called Joe Booth were the leadership team for that and we managed to effect enough change so that it was the first FIFA game in four years to gain Metacritic points – the review website used by the gaming industry. That was the way the company measured success. Obviously, sales were one aspect and Metacritic was another.

"It wasn't necessarily that I was hired to rescue anything, but the company had obviously seen that they needed to do some things differently. They'd started a new engine, and were looking for new faces, direction and ideas.

"I don't remember exactly the market share when I joined, but I know that it was a struggle. I'm pretty sure it was around 50-50 between FIFA and PES. Most of the people that were brought in at that time were from the UK, and we were all Pro Evo fans.

"In 2003, FIFA had tried to do a couple of things differently. They tried to free the ball up a little, and it made a difference but it didn't really make an impact on Pro Evo in terms of quality. We had to make huge changes.

"Also, when we rewrote the engine for the PS3 and Xbox 360 era, there was a change in attitude and design philosophy – going for much more systemic game mechanics, rather than the scripted mechanics we'd used in the past.

"The result of those things was that we created a much more dynamic game in terms of depth and variety that was truer to real football.

"So, with scripting, a header animation was two people locked into it – one person started a jump, the other hadn't, and it was always pre-determined who would win that header.

"We moved to a much more logical, systemic solution, where people chose to jump whenever they wanted to. If there was a contact then we'd resolve that with forces, weight, aggression and heading ability. That obviously felt much better to play.

"One of the first things we did was base the shooting system on real life. So we looked at different factors that would affect the result of a shot – was he off balance; was he under pressure; was he jostling; was the ball coming across his body; was it bouncing; what was its lateral velocity?

"We looked at all these different contexts and factors and said, in real life, if that was the scenario, how would the player most likely hit the ball? In this scenario, he'd most likely mis-hit it by hitting the left-hand side of the ball because he mis-timed it. Or, in another scenario, he'd get under the ball and it'd go over the bar.

"Doing that created emergent moments within the gameplay, and that was the path we took – a shift in design philosophy and the company's focus around FIFA. They invested heavily in gameplay as they'd realised that was what mattered and the results came."

That's putting it mildly. What Paterson witnessed, under his guidance, was a huge swing in popularity for *FIFA* – with critics raving about the new gameplay experience he'd helped to implement. Slowly, but surely, *PES* was reined in.

"FIFA 07, for me, was really big. It was the first FIFA that increased our Metacritic score. FIFA 08 increased by ten points, then FIFA 09 was only up five points but we knew we were onto something, because people around the company had started to play it at that point, on their lunch break. FIFA 10 was where we really got excited, as we hit 90 on Metacritic, which was the goal all along – that was the Holy Grail for us.

"That's where we started to gain the momentum. You can be beating Pro Evo, but it takes a while before the consumers sit up and take notice, especially in the mainland European countries. I think Italy and France were two of the last bastions of Pro Evo. I suppose it's like switching from Manchester United to Manchester City – it very rarely happens, so when it does it takes a long time.

"At that time, Pro Evo had the Master League mode, which was a stronger experience than our career mode, so we had to invest heavily in that in FIFA 11 to 13. And on FIFA 12 we put Online Season play on and the momentum continued to grow, which was much more compelling than what we had before."

From a position of panic and fear, with *FIFA* trailing *PES* by some distance in 2004, the balance had tilted in the opposite direction by the end of the decade – *Pro Evolution Soccer*'s reign was over.

It was a transformation that would have seemed impossible at the time of Gary Paterson's arrival at EA – though the influx of Brits and Europeans at that time did demand some persuasive pitching, as many of the staff headhunted were reticent about the switch.

David Rutter, now a leading figure on *FIFA*, admits his own disdain for EA prior to working for the company: "Previous to joining EA, I worked for a bunch of different video games companies, starting from 1995, and have only really ever made football games.

"Coming here, for a lot of people, was this weird double-life: when it came to EA you were one of two mindsets, you were either a video gamer who thought they suck, or you were the businessy kind of person who thought they were a brilliant company to work for.

"I was certainly the former, and a lot of people took some convincing to come and work here, from the period of time when I started. To put things in perspective, we have more than 20 nationalities working on the game, most of whom were imported to join the team between 2005 and 2008.

"It was a big transformation that happened here, when we went from lots of marketing, lots of glitz and glamour, lots of licenses but not a particularly great game to deciding we're going to make a really good video game to match the budget that was being spent on everything else.

"They hired in the best in the world at what they did and brought them to a beautiful city and great facility to work on a team that, previous to that, had been tasked with making a football game and didn't really get it."

*

The first *PES* proper emerged in 2001 and was immediately pitched as the underdog rival to *FIFA* – minus the official licenses or financial might of their rival, with the east versus west dynamic an interesting undercurrent.

PES 5 was the market leader – signified by Henry's switching of allegiance – and its successor saw more licenses added to Konami's stable, with deals in place for international kits, plus France's Ligue 1, but various messy wrangles saw them lose the rights to the Bundesliga, while Chelsea also disappeared. Serbia and Montenegro remained in the game despite the nation being dissolved some months before release, while Arsenal's and Bayern Munich's stadium moves hadn't been reflected virtually.

PES 7, better known as *Pro Evolution Soccer 2008*, starred Cristiano Ronaldo on the game cover, and it was Lionel Messi who starred on 2009's version, which also had the Champions League license, as Konami really took the game to EA. However, the tide was in the process of turning – *FIFA* was developing rapidly and now it was *PES* playing catch up.

One new feature in *PES 8* proved to be game changing, although it would be *FIFA* that enjoyed the most success from it. The Become a Legend mode followed the progress of a single player's entire career, and would go on to inspire *FIFA 08*'s massively popular Be a Pro mode.

From that point, *PES* was a distant second to *FIFA*; the 2010 game underwent a huge overhaul to try and match their rival, a radical and desperate move. Off field, licenses continued to come – Europa League in 2010, the Copa Libertadores and UEFA Super Cup in 2011 – but had little impact on its share of the market. By then, EA's hunger to be the best was really showing.

So, it was inevitable that, in 2012, *PES* lost their star signing – EA swooping to poach Lionel Messi for their *FIFA 13* cover. It must have been a satisfyingly sweet moment, serving up a taste of Konami's own medicine to their rivals, after Thierry Henry absconded seven years earlier.

*

That wasn't the first footballing video game feud that *FIFA* had experienced, having first entered the genre as the underdogs, playing second fiddle, very briefly, to then market leader *Sensible Soccer*.

It's a time that Matt Webster – one of the few current members of the EA team that worked on the first *FIFA* game – remembers fondly. He said: "We were going head-to-head. We wanted to beat Sensi, but they were an entrenched competitor – they had the brand awareness, everyone knew what Sensible Soccer was.

"But, from the US point of view, the people at EA didn't understand football at the time, really. No one did. When I was still based in the UK, working on the first game, we used to videotape Match of the Day and send it to Canada.

"We were saying 'you can't call this EA Soccer, surely it'd make sense to go to the governing body?' So I found the name of Keith Cooper, who was FIFA's spokesperson, and it was all pretty amateur at the time. We ended up doing the deal, but we got nothing really apart from the name.

"North America, at the time, with the World Cup coming up, was a real challenge. I remember reading some of the hare-brained ideas come up with by the American sports consultants – like having two balls on the pitch, getting rid of throw-ins and the offside rule – so we needed to go over there and educate those guys on football."

Webster arrived in Canada to work on the game, and his presence on the other side of the world proved serendipitous, as a late-night spot of procrastination averted what would have been a glaring error – and a bad start for a new video game franchise.

He laughed: "I remember being holed up in this hotel in Burnaby for three or four months. It was right opposite the office, but it was horrible, so I preferred spending time in the office than going back to my room.

"We had just submitted the final version of the game and we were in a rush because we wanted to get it out. I booted the game up at about 2am and I looked at the title screen and had to blink a few times – there was a f***ing spelling mistake. And it had been there forever. We'd written 'licensed by Sega Entepises'. We'd missed the 'r'.

"And there was no-one around. We didn't have mobile phones then, so I had to try and find a way to call people and wake them up, and then go and pick them up in cars to get someone to change the text and resubmit a version for Europe."

That instance alone makes Webster a legendary member of the *FIFA* team – an all-star lineup that makes them the Real Madrid of the gaming world…

How each release sounded

For many, past iterations of *FIFA* have become as memorable for their soundtracks as their actual content. While the gameplay of many versions can blend into each other, the theme music for many *FIFA* games are evocative of a certain time and place – Blur's *Song 2*, for instance, was unmistakably the sound of *FIFA: Road to World Cup 98*, a song that looped constantly in my household – much to my parents' dismay, no doubt.

Here, we take a stroll down memory lane, revisiting the tracks that featured on each game in the *FIFA* series.

FIFA International Soccer

The groundbreaking first release included five generic, arcade-y tracks – as did its successor, *FIFA 95*. Though neither had any words, they were well pitched, catchy beats.

FIFA 96

This release trebled the playlist, with 15 songs composed and arranged by George Coleman.

FIFA 97

Featured ten songs composed by EA Sports – though one was a 'joke song', featuring excerpts from John Motson's commentary, and not included on the PC version. On the PlayStation edition, the hidden song would appear as 'Track 6'. All very mysterious.

FIFA: Road to World Cup 98

The first release to have a 'title track' – which was the aforementioned *Song 2*, by Blur.

There were also five other songs on the game – four from The Crystal Method and a track by Electric Skychurch. But no one remembers those.

FIFA 99

This year's title track was *The Rockafeller Skank (Remix)* by Fat Boy Slim, which charted in various countries around the world – reaching number 6 in the UK charts, and entering the US Billboard Hot 100.

FIFA 2000

It's Only Us, by Robbie Williams, was the title song of 2000, with various other tracks featured on the game including *Stop The Rock* by Apollo 440, and *All About Beats (DJ Scissoricks Mix)* by Junior Blanks.

FIFA 2001

2001's title track was *Bodyrock* by Moby, which sneaked into the UK's official Top 40, at number 38.

FIFA Football 2002

British group Gorillaz topped 2002's playlist with *19-2000 (Soulchild Remix)*, while future megastar DJ Tiesto was the standout name from the rest of the playlist.

FIFA Football 2003

To Get Down (Fatboy Slim Remix) by Timo Maas was the title track, in the first year of EA Trax, giving the game a stellar soundtrack. It also announced Avril Lavigne and Ms. Dynamite-ee to the world.

FIFA Football 2004

Kings of Leon were next to be given an international platform, as their song *Red Morning Light* was named title track. Elsewhere, Brazilian band Tribalistas enjoyed huge success from their song *Ja Sei Namorar* featuring on the game – charting in various nations around the world, earning them the best-selling album of the year in Portugal, going triple platinum in Italy, double platinum in Spain, and resulting in a nomination for the BBC Awards for World Music. Not bad.

FIFA Football 2005

No set title song, but a 38-track playlist including *Fit But You Know It* by The Streets. The Scissor Sisters' achieved international success with *Take Your Mama* fuelled by its placement in the game – and Swiss band Manana were subsequently signed by EMI.

FIFA 06

With Bloc Party being fans of *FIFA*, there was a beneficial opportunity for all parties involved – and their song *Helicopter* was the title track for this release, with the video premiere coinciding with the game's launch. Somali singer K'naan was also on the playlist, going on his first European tour after the game's release.

The in-game sound system from *FIFA 06* – as music grew in prevalence.

FIFA 07

You might not remember *FIFA 07's* title track from its name – *Can't Get Enough (Mekon Remix)* by The Infadels – but a quick blast on *YouTube* should remind you. Also signed for the game were Keane, whose song *Nothing In My Way* was part of a key spell of success for the British band. They topped the charts with their debut album a few months before the game launched.

FIFA 08

The title track for this game was *Sketches (20 Something Life)* by La Rocca, while The Hoosiers' song *Goodbye Mr A* would be the first time *FIFA* was product-placed in a music video – another demonstration of the brand's increasing global recognition and power.

FIFA 09

The game's title track was *Let U Know* by Plastilina Mosh, but the show was stolen by Hot Chip's *Ready For The Floor (Soulwax Remix)*, which became an international sensation, and was nominated for a Grammy award that year.

FIFA 10

Nothing to Worry About by Peter Bjorn and John was *FIFA 10*'s lead song, though EA might have felt more pride around *Be Somebody* by The Enemy – as the video was EA's concept, and produced by the company. It became the official video, filmed at the Ricoh Arena, as The Enemy played as special guests on Oasis' final tour.

FIFA 11

No title song, but 33 tracks including songs by Linkin Park, Massive Attack and We Are Scientists.

FIFA 12

Kids by Sleigh Bells is the title track, but Brits Chase & Status also feature.

FIFA 13

Kasabian, one of the most prolific bands in terms of *FIFA* appearances, had the title track with *Club Foot*.

FIFA 14

No title song, but 37 tracks including songs by Wretch 32, Disclosure and Nine Inch Nails. Brit singer John Newman's breakthrough song *Love Me Again* was a personal favourite on the playlist.

FIFA 15

No title song, but 41 tracks including Kwabs' breakthrough song *Walk* – which catapulted him to huge international success, and led to him supporting Sam Smith on his global tour in the aftermath of the game's release.

A potted history of how an 'experiment' became a behemoth

You regard it today as the world's biggest sports video game franchise, an unstoppable series that commands recognition and respect the world over. But it wasn't always that way. Here are the key dates in FIFA's history – how it started off small, before becoming a global giant.

1982 Electronic Arts is founded by Trip Hawkins, leaving Apple Inc. to do so. Initially, it was known as Amazin' Software, but that was ditched.

1983 Hawkins decides to package his products in square CD-style boxes with 'album art' on the front. This fitted in with EA's philosophy to celebrate their developers as rock stars.

1984 Having been rejected by his favourite NFL player, Joe Montana, Hawkins agrees an endorsement deal with retired coach John Madden, who envisions it as an educational tool. It is released four years later.

1991 Hawkins transitions from EA to form a new console platform, the 3DO – short for three-dimensional operating system. Despite being founded in partnership with the likes of LG, Panasonic and, of course, EA, the firm went bankrupt in 2003, without major success.

1991 On the back of Madden's popularity, and subsequent releases in Golf and Ice Hockey, the Electronic Arts Sports Network, known as EASN, is formed, as a sports branch of the by now successful EA.

1993 The company's first soccer title, *FIFA International Soccer*, debuts and, against all expectations, proves an immediate success story.

1995 *FIFA 96* is the first title in the series to use real player names, after securing the FIFPro license to their rights. This was a significant early step to attracting gamers, despite fierce competition elsewhere.

1997 An early sighting of the depth EA Sports would strive towards, as *FIFA: Road to World Cup 98* game secures the long-desired World Cup rights, and celebrates by including all 172 FIFA-registered national teams.

2000 *FIFA 2001* is the first game in the series that can be played online, on the PC.

2010 The *FIFA* series reaches more than 100 million sales, confirming its role as the biggest-selling sports game on the market – as well as EA Sports' most profitable game.

2012 EA make a big signing, that of Lionel Messi as cover star. The Argentine previously served the same role for rivals *Pro Evolution Soccer*.

2013 Released in 2012, *FIFA 13* now becomes the best-selling sports video game in history, selling more than eight million copies.

2015 EA announce that female teams will be added to *FIFA* for the first time, with 12 of the women's national teams from the 2015 World Cup playable in the new game.

Part Two

How The Game
is Made

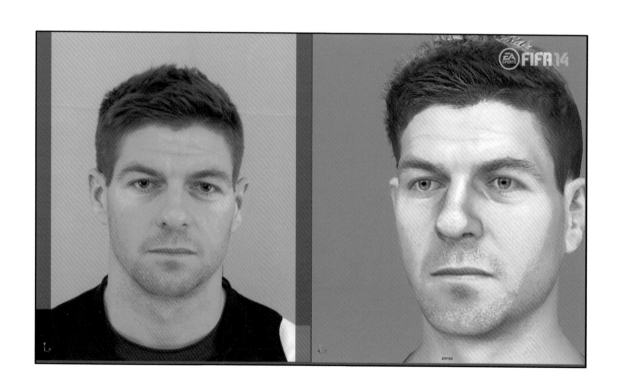

① CHENKO4

CUT TO

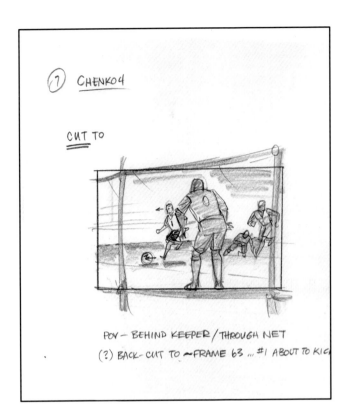

POV — BEHIND KEEPER / THROUGH NET
(?) BACK-CUT TO ~FRAME 63 ... #1 ABOUT TO KIC[

③ CHENKO 4

(~FRAME 54)

PLAYERS CONTINUE TOWARD CAMERA.
#2 DEFENSE TRIES TACKLE & MISSES ...

4. FIFA's Ultimate Team – the people who put the game together

EA Sports' line up of superstars, whose chemistry, clearly, is 100

Given the hero worship usually attributed and applied to the footballers at the centre of *FIFA* and, in particular, with their varying levels of rarity, Ultimate Team, we decided that it would only be fair to give some of the people behind the scenes a little sip of that adulation too.

Though most of the men – yes, sorry, gaming remains a male-dominated industry – interviewed for this section were, at best, uneasy with the idea of their face appearing on a mock-up of a FUT card and, at worst, baffled by the prospect, it seems only fitting that this XI of geniuses and innovators get some credit.

After all, this is the team of people that have put together the best loved football game in the world – from the man who casually dreamt up Ultimate Team and watched as it skyrocketed into *FIFA*'s best mode, to members of the original team who worked on *FIFA International Soccer*, via a Jamaican international footballer who ended up working on the biggest stage of the virtual game instead.

In each instance, the key 'players' have a team logo on their card. This hasn't been randomly or arbitrarily assigned – this is the team they support. Likewise, their national flag is accurate, too.

We didn't go down the route of assigning them specific *FIFA*-related stats such as pace and power, for fear of causing an office ruckus. Guys, you're all equal in our eyes.

Some of these characters you'll see recurring throughout the rest of the book, while others offered a bit of insight into their journey to EA – including one who ended up in Vancouver after a detour from Pakistan. This section also includes some of their highlights, from being recognised by a 'fan', to putting in a man of the match performance in front of a packed Highbury crowd.

This, ladies and gentlemen, is *FIFA*'s Ultimate Team. You see what we did there..?

1. Gary Paterson. The Scot genius joined EA in August 2004, moving onto the gameplay team for *FIFA 07*. He was recruited from Codemasters after his work on *LMA Manager* and was initially appointed to further the *FIFA Manager 06* spin-off series, before promptly being moved onto the main title.

As well as radicalising the fortunes of a game struggling against rival *Pro Evolution Soccer*, Gary also provided another, less vaunted addition to *FIFA* – his younger brother.

He admitted: "I made Andrew a referee for one version. His mates would wind him up saying he had a terrible game."

2. Matt Prior. "I had a weird route to EA. I'm sure a lot of people moved to Canada to work for them, but I didn't even know it was here.

"Before this, I was an expedition leader with a company based in England who built a truck and drove from London to Beijing and back again – I met my wife on one of the legs of that trip, in Pakistan, and she was from Vancouver.

"Eventually, I'd had enough of sleeping in a tent, and moved here to marry her, with no notion that *FIFA* was made here. I'd played it all my life, but you just think it's made in England.

"I saw an advert in the local paper that they were hiring for QA testers, really the ground floor level, so joined and worked my way up – which is one of the good things about EA, you can climb up.

"Back then, as an industry, there were no courses you could go on and things like that, so it was more a passion for gaming and sport that got you there. QA is a bit of a brutal job so you absolutely have to have a passion to do that job; it proves your commitment, so to speak."

Despite that unorthodox start to life in games, Prior is the man behind *FIFA*'s most successful mode, Ultimate Team, inspired by his playground nostalgia – getting it first into a Champions League spin-off, before revolutionising the main FIFA game, too.

"Swapsies is a part of a football fan's DNA, and I always thought it would be great to take it into the digital world. It was a lot of work to do, and it was a bit of a risk, so it took a lot of convincing that first time, and then when we put it into the main FIFA too.

"My reason for suggesting it for the main series was because the event title didn't get it out there enough – it was like an Indie film, a lot of people liked it and loved it but it just didn't get that broad exposure. We didn't renew the Champions League license that year, and we were looking for DLC instead, so the worlds kind of aligned and the rest is history.

"As soon as we did it, the forums lit up, and we got a sense of the potential of what it was going to become. We saw the appetite for it early on."

3. Aaron McHardy. "I played football professionally for the majority of my life, in and around North America and the Caribbean. I also played for Jamaica internationally, at Under 21, Under 23, and once for the full team.

"I played striker for Jamaica, but for my entire career elsewhere I was a central midfielder. When I showed up, they had a good midfield but were struggling to score goals at the time. I came in and scored in my first five games, so me and Ricardo Fuller were fighting for the same position.

"I had a lot of work permit issues trying to play professionally. I had a couple of clubs in England that wanted to sign me, but I couldn't meet the criteria – your nation have to be in the top 75 in the world and you have to have played 75% of your full internationals over the last two years.

"By the time I was about 25, I was living out of Vancouver. I had a friend David Griffiths – a Trinidadian international – who recommended me to the team that were making FIFA Street to come in and do motion capture for them, as a local talent. I got on with the guys, and got a job in QA testing FIFA. Eventually, I pitched a feature, Skill Moves, to the development team, and they liked it, and they brought me on to make FIFA 08."

If that journey to *FIFA* key man is unlikely, his support for Arsenal is slightly more predictable – inspired by a moment of genius by a famous former Gunner. He said: "I was actually born in Vancouver – my father was of Jamaican descent, and I lived there for a part of my life – watching football on Saturdays. We only had a round-up show, without full matches most of the time, apart from the FA Cup finals.

"Certain teams would get featured – Juventus, Real Madrid, Manchester United – and that's who we'd choose from. I went the path of Arsenal. I was playing for a provincial team in British Columbia, and we travelled to the Ian Rush tournament in the UK and, while we were there, we got to go to the Charity Shield, which was Manchester United versus Arsenal.

"In that game, I was young and impressionable, about 12-years old, and my father was already cheering for Arsenal. So, when Ian Wright scored a scissor kick in extra time to win it, that was it for me – I was Arsenal."

4. Santiago Jaramillo. "I'm a producer, but one that wears many different hats. I did gameplay exclusively until FIFA 12, and then from 13 onwards I've been doing career mode, miscellaneous stuff like the FIFA Trainer this year, localisation, and all the broadcast side of things.

"When I was growing up in Colombia in the mid-90s, the league that was shown the most was the Italian Serie A, and my favourite player was Gianfranco Zola, with Parma at the time. When Chelsea bought him, I followed him, and started watching them.

"Then, a few years later, Abramovich took over and a bunch of money came in and it's a different team now, but I was following them before that happened.

"Every time you say you're a Chelsea fan you have to say you were a fan before Abramovich, otherwise you fall into a different category."

5. David Rutter. Something of a games industry celebrity, Rutter admitted that he was slightly star struck to share a stage with Pele at a 2015 preview of *FIFA 16*: "Being on stage with Pele was so cool, although I got some terrible photos – please don't use them, I looked like a right muppet.

"I've only been recognised properly once. It was after E3 in Los Angeles, in the Duty Free shop buying a bottle of gin, which is one of my wife's and my tipples of choice, after a stressful week.

"A guy came up to me and said 'You're David Rutter!' I was dazzled, it was the first time it had happened to me, and I turned to the woman who was serving me and went 'I've just been recognised, in Los Angeles, this is so cool'.

"And she said: 'I'm sorry, sir, but your credit card has just been declined' – humiliated in front of the only fan I've ever had."

David's lifestyle in Vancouver still revolves around *FIFA*, and sounds idyllic: "Saturday mornings are great for me here, because I get up before the kids get up, and have a huge number of TV channels; I can watch whichever Premier League game I want. I sit there and I pick the fixtures that are going to be the most entertaining games, and enjoy football for football's sake.

"I still play the game every day, I'm still relatively good at it – I play at home and at work, against the guys. Because that's what we do. People say 'what a brilliant job, you get to play games all year', which is true, but you get to play *one game* all year. And, sometimes, it's atrocious because, when we're building it, we're breaking things to make them better.

"But, at this time of year, when the game's basically finished, there'll be a tweak put in for one thing and everyone will pile in with complaints. They changed passing very slightly last Wednesday and I just freaked out, because I couldn't pass any more and it was driving me mad.

"Then, all of a sudden, I was back to winning ways. You have those moments of 'you've completely broken it'."

6. Jan Tian   7. Adam Shaikh   8. Nick Channon

9. Matthew Webster. "For my first football game, my father took me to White Hart Lane for Tottenham versus Manchester United, when I was seven-years-old, in the late Seventies, but he had tickets in the away end and you can't exactly cheer for the home team in the away end.

"So that was that. One of my best football memories came from working on FIFA – for FIFA 95, the UK launch event was at a Manchester United versus Arsenal game at Highbury.

"We had a match on the pitch at half-time, and I ended up scoring a hat trick, with the crowd really getting behind me. It was incredible."

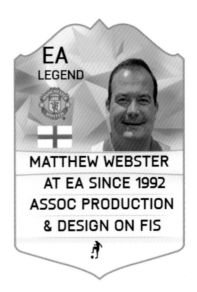

EA
LEGEND

MATTHEW WEBSTER
AT EA SINCE 1992
ASSOC PRODUCTION
& DESIGN ON FIS

EA
STAR

SEBASTIAN ENRIQUE
AT EA SINCE 2005
GEN 4
LEAD PRODUCER

10. Sebastian Enrique. "I started programming on the day after high school as an intern. I always wanted to work in games, but I would need a sponsor for the visa, etc. So, after finishing my degree, I applied for PhDs in the US to get into the industry.

"I did an internship with Microsoft in Redmond, and during the second year I was tired of the PhD, so got a job at EA. I started as a software engineer, then I started doing more design and moved to production.

"I love doing what I do – the same love and passion I had from day one I have today. My first gig was doing the demos for PS2. I had to burn the disc myself because there wasn't a media lab or anything, and I had no clue how to develop on PS2 at that time.

"The new generation of consoles is a big change, there's so much more power. For me, the Xbox 360 looked like PS2. The new generation of consoles allow us to have more CPU processing for better AI and graphics. Things we are doing now we could only dream of before."

Clearly fond of the job he does, Sebastian is also quite keen on the place he now calls home: "Vancouver is a beautiful place, very safe, and every time I stress I just take a kayak or drive to the mountains, and that's relaxing. If you're in a city like Buenos Aires, it's impossible to do that.

"And the office is the best. I've been to multiple game studios and this is the best. I used to play football twice a week on the pitch, and do yoga. It's a beautiful place to work. I do miss my family and lifetime friends, back home in Buenos Aires, but working here for EA is a dream."

EA
LEGEND

CHIP LANGE
AT EA SINCE 1991
MARKETING
GURU

11. Chip Lange. "FIFA is all my kids play – they're on Ultimate Team every free minute they possibly can. They learn the sport of soccer through it, and all have favourite players – Zlatan Ibrahimovic is not someone my kids would have on their jersey otherwise.

"We wake up Saturday and Sunday mornings and watch the Premier League and have all become fans. We actually flew home from vacation to watch the Barcelona – Manchester United game when they were here, so our whole family has got kind of obsessed with it.

"One of the things I used to pride myself on – when we were making the game – was that I could beat the guys in development. But my kids have long since surpassed me.

"My favourite team is Crystal Palace and the reason is I had a buddy who relocated from the UK working on my team, so we made a blood pact that he could be a San Francisco 49ers fan for life, and I would adopt his team in the UK – Palace. We exchanged jerseys and I root for Palace not to get relegated.

"My son is a big Everton fan because he loves Tim Howard; my eldest son is a PSG fan because of Ibrahimovic, who he thinks is the greatest player ever; and then my little guy is a fan of Chelsea, because they won something. He's little, and they were the best.

"But the Barcelona world tour certainly sold us jerseys, and we've got a Neymar fathead in one of my kids' rooms."

Inside the hub of EA Sports, their main HQ in Vancouver, Canada

Hidden away between mountain peaks and the longest river in British Columbia, a 15 minute drive from central Vancouver, is the sleepy area of Burnaby. It's a place with a strong East Asian demographic, and perhaps best known as the birthplace of actor Michael J. Fox and cheesy crooner Michael Bublé. To find it as the home of video game football is quite unexpected.

In a continent where professional soccer stars can (generally) walk around unrecognised, and without interference, EA Sports have adopted a similarly anonymous setting for *FIFA* HQ. It allows them to float under the radar between releases. If the surrounding areas to the headquarters are relatively silent, inside there's a low, constant hum of productivity. This is a place where work gets done.

From the outside, the HQ looks like a luxury-gated community, with the main building protruding and guarded by a nondescript security entrance. Its true identity is only given away by an EA logo on the side of the road.

This base is a 400,000 square foot campus of innovation, where *FIFA* is developed alongside *UFC* and *NHL*. Amongst the facilities here are video editing suites, music composition areas and full-size theatres for presentations to visiting delegates.

As you arrive at the main entrance, various motivational monikers hang from the ceiling, such as 'act with integrity', 'be accountable', 'learn and grow' and 'think gamer first'. Walking down a tube-shaped glass tunnel takes visitors and staff alike to the main reception, kitted out with sofas and, of course, games consoles playing their titles.

A large iPad offers a rolling information screen with staff deals on local aquarium tickets, parking restriction reminders, encouragement to recycle and a 'welcome to our team' message for newcomers. Behind it is a small store, EA Experience, selling branded merchandise and various games from the company's back catalogue.

Filtering through are the hundreds of staff who work here on a daily basis, sporting a relaxed dress code, with shorts, baseball caps and dogs all common. One chap even walks through carrying rollerblades.

Beyond the main security door of reception – an area which only approved visitors can reach – is an arcade games room to the immediate left, offering free-to-play classics such as

Street Fighter II: Champion Edition, and baseball game *World Series 99*. There's also a Metallica-themed pinball machine.

An EA employee makes use of the free-to-play arcade room.

Just past the arcade room is the entrance to the canteen, "EAt" (yes, spelled that way), outside of which is a coffee shop and leisure area, comprising several sofas and three huge screens showing live sport. Inside the canteen, the choice of food on offer is astonishing – there are separate counters for burgers, pizzas, pan Asian food, sushi, sandwiches and salad.

In the wrap-selling area, there's an option titled 'The Andrew Wilson' after the EA Sports CEO, which is chicken, avocado, tomatoes, red relish and a tortilla. And delicious, in case you wondered.

Upstairs, in the office area, there are signed shirts hanging from brown rails dotted across the ceiling to facilitate their display. In one member of staff's office alone, there are personalised dedications from Lionel Messi, José Mourinho and the entire Liverpool squad.

I visited on a Monday, and live *Monday Night Football* from the Premier League is being watched avidly from the desks of most staff members, as the teams kick off at midday, Canada time. Though there's plenty more to watch from this office.

Corner rooms offer stunning panoramic views of North Vancouver – from the mountainous horizon in the distance, to the city skyline in the middle-distance and a forest of trees that border the secluded EA complex.

EA staff peruse lunch options in the canteen of their Burnaby headquarters.

The offices also overlook a five-a-side football pitch, which plays host to competitive lunch break matches and is also used for some specialised motion capture footage. Alongside the pitch is a basketball court – which can also host roller hockey – and a beach volleyball pitch complete with sand. Elsewhere on the campus is a well-stocked library, several video game rooms, more coffee bars, a high-level fitness centre and several outside patios on which to watch the sport below, or simply catch some rays.

Weekly visits are arranged from barbers and tailors, so that staff can worry about one less thing in their personal lives, with their work being such a dominant focus. The studio also provides concierge services like dry cleaning, and even a doggy daycare centre.

The HQs for companies such as Google, Apple and Facebook are often raved about, but EA Sports' Canadian campus must list alongside each of them – it's difficult to imagine any employee having qualms or complaints about the facilities on offer.

At lunchtimes, the cafeteria is a busy meeting and eating spot, providing a vast choice of meals – from seafood to vegan, Asian to Italian, carb-free to gluten-free. Everything about EAC has been developed with a social element in mind, with employees' welfare outside of their immediate line of work clearly an important factor. And, by making the studio a place that people want to be, it ensures the workforce arrive at the office earlier and leave later.

Adam Shaikh, the Creative Director of FUT, allows an insight into the social side of the campus, by revealing that he's part of the lunchtime five-a-side league and acknowledging the way that football permeates his day-to-day life: "Football's great. It creates such a passionate environment – we have a rec league, we have matches going on at lunchtime. It's a lot of fun and a privilege to work on one of the world's great titles.

A lunchtime match takes place on the EA Sports pitch.

"I've got two little children, and the eldest one is just starting to play now, and I'm getting my wife more into football, so we all get up in the morning and watch the matches together. When you love doing something for work, it's never a trial and that sort of infectious attitude carries wherever. If I'm at home, talking excitedly about it, my wife's excited too.

"The biggest thing about working on FIFA is just the size. It's a massive team, not only within our group, but it's in multiple locations, there's all parts of EA we touch as well. Just on the scale, it's incredible. Even from my own perspective, I'm the main creative director for *one* mode in FIFA."

That passion for the sport is a key adhesive for the various teams based at Burnaby, who often come from wildly different backgrounds. Football, as in many walks of life, proves a valuable icebreaker for EA employees, who can often have very little else in common.

Nick Channon, Senior Producer on *FIFA*, says: "It's a global game and operation, with bases in Romania and Germany, too. On the team itself we have over 20 nationalities, so it's pretty diverse. My line producer is Argentinean, for instance, which gives a different flavour and influence – I grew up watching the English game, not South American football.

"I play FIFA at home, and I think we all do – at the end of the day you make video games because you want to. It's a tough job, it's long hours, but for us most people will play it outside of work too, as massive football fans. It's no different to people who play our game, really – but maybe not quite as much as the hardcore.

"Living in Canada, we actually get more football than you do in the UK, because we get the 3pm games on a Saturday, and everyone on the team watches, so there's always something every week you see, which you think would be pretty cool."

One staff member's impressive haul of signed memorabilia.

And it's not just football fans you'll bump into in the corridors of EAC, there are some ex-professionals there, too, with EA Sports specifically seeking out experienced individuals for their gameplay team, to add an air of authenticity to key decision making.

Senior Gameplay Producer Aaron McHardy explained the benefits: "We have a lot of experts on the team that have played football professionally, so we rely on them – we watch a lot of videos. When that's not sufficient, we have access to people in the professional world who can give us the inside stuff we need.

"I played professionally, and for Jamaica internationally, but couldn't get a work permit to play in Europe, so ended up joining EA as a QA tester and working my way up. In days gone by, when I was in QA, we lived in a different part of the building, and it was mystical if one of the producers came downstairs – but we've been working over the years to have our QA sat with us and become part of the team."

*

One of the many perks of working at EA's Burnaby headquarters – which definitely has the air of a university campus when walking around it – is, reportedly, being cut off slightly from the rest of the footballing world, by both distance and time difference. That's according to VP and GM David Rutter, who thinks it's important that staff don't get caught up in the success of the series.

He said: "Before you work on a big triple-A title, you don't know what success means. I have worked on games that have sold very little and thought they had done really well – then you come to EA and all of a sudden multiple millions of sales are normal.

"When I joined, we were in the process of launching FIFA 08, and when people were talking about sales numbers for that game, they were saying 'a few million'. As the following years came, we saw how millions of sales were catching up with the number of the game that was being made – FIFA 10 was aiming at ten million.

**Screens at the canteen's entrance show live sport,
including from the Premier League. That's Petr Cech up there.**

"So you have to look around and compare yourselves to other things in the world. My kids love Taylor Swift – how many records does she sell? Or how many people go and watch a movie? And you realise that you aren't just making a video game, it's 'mainstream entertainment', and that's a different kettle of fish when you get to that scale.

"But we're so distant from it that we don't really notice it. We're away from the big Oxford Street launch or shops turned into FIFA. We don't ever see any of that – we're lucky if we see a single poster.

"You look at the popularity of the sport, just generally around the world, and it's massively more popular here in North America than it ever was. Women's soccer over here is enormous, and you combine that with lots of people now having consoles.

"I'm quite proud of the fact that there's no murder, no swearing in the game – well, on the screen, I know a lot of people do a lot of swearing when they're playing the game – but it is a relatively wholesome experience. On the one hand, we have the entertainment that that provides, but also the stimulation for people to get out there and play a bit of football too."

Inside EA's high tech Motion Capture studio.

Probably the most impressive part of EAC, aside from the leisure options, is EA Sports' state of the art motion capture studio, which is one of the biggest and best equipped of its kind on the planet. It plays host to over 200 shoot days every year, producing more than half a million seconds of animation, recorded by more than 50 cameras. Amongst those being captured are sport's most stellar names – from Lionel Messi to Rory McIlroy, via LeBron James and various NFL All Stars.

While the rest of EAC is open-plan and well-lit, the motion capture area has a very different feel to it – with all outside light and noises blocked off. Stepping inside is like walking into a theatre stage's spotlight, with nothing else really visible in the great darkness beyond. Instead of being watched by theatre goers, though, you are observed by crowds of cameras, following your every movement and action.

For the players, such as Messi or the female stars observed for the addition of women's teams to *FIFA 16*, EA has more than 5,000 square feet of artificial turf, which wouldn't be out of place at any of the world's top stadiums and can be used inside the motion capture studio, as well as out. Increasingly, the facility needs to be able to go portable to fit into the schedules of the superstars they work with – Messi, for instance, has a diary generally booked up months in advance. Similarly, NHL stars need to do their motion capture work on ice.

The MoCap technology captures Gareth Bale in full flow.

*

EA Sports have two UK bases, one of which is in Guildford – where press presentations and hands-on sessions are held for media from across Europe. The grey nondescript building in which the company is set is a short stroll from the train station, and wouldn't make you look twice if you walked past it. Like EAC in Burnaby, this is a low-key setting.

Inside, the office houses HR, recruitment and PR staff. On one wall is a motif listing 'leadership competencies' for the staff, which include 'Be Human' – an interesting core value for a business involved in such a lucrative industry, but testament to the company's success. Although not quite on par with the staggering facilities on offer in Vancouver, EA look after their Guildford group, too – with a swish gym that hosts regular classes for staff, while various cafe areas mimic Burnaby's magnificent cafeteria, albeit on a smaller scale.

It's this office that plays host to a special media day for post-E3 announcements around significant *FIFA 16* developments – and, notably, Ultimate Team. When I visit, a handful of journalists in the room are the first in the world, outside of EA, to see the trailer for FUT

Draft, at that point still unfinished, subject to further filming with Gary Neville and Jamie Carragher. Hosting the presentation are Nick Channon and Adam Shaikh, flown in from Canada to brief the European media.

EA's other UK base is, surprisingly, in Macclesfield – which, like Guildford's proximity to London, is on the outskirts of Manchester. This is the home of British company Chillingo – bought by EA in 2010 for almost $20million in cash, having published iPhone and iPad hits like *Angry Birds* and *Cut The Rope*.

The deal was fuelled by a desire from EA Sports to up the ante with their mobile and social offerings, eager to be amongst the market leaders on modern platforms like Facebook and Apple, just as they have been on their traditional counterparts – the games consoles. Similarly, a year prior to the purchase of Chillingo, EA had spent $400million on Playfish, the Facebook specialists. Explaining the deal, EA's official website gives another mention to their 'human' focus, writing: "Chillingo has grown over time, but one thing never changes: their human touch. Chillingo considers developer friends as part of the family, and ensure a level of trust and understanding that you won't find elsewhere."

Such purchases would have been made in complete confidence, having enjoyed success from the 2006 takeover of Swedish developer DICE (Digital Illusions Creative Entertainment). That deal came after the success of the *Battlefield* franchise from DICE – a title which would go on to become one of EA's biggest, along with the ground-breaking Frostbite engine developed in Stockholm; initially developed for *Battlefield*, it is now used for various EA titles.

Another European arm of the flagship studio in Canada is in Bucharest, Romania – where a group of engineers, artists and designers work on the *FIFA* series. Among them is the Testing Division, which offers quality assurances for EA's range of games on their multiple platforms, fine-tuning the specifics for porting between console and mobile, say.

Interestingly, on EA's official website, an insight into the social culture of the Bucharest team – known as EA Romania – is offered: "We love our parties! Whether in the middle of the year (the summer party) or at the end (the Christmas party) we like to have fun! What better way to cool off in the middle of the summer than playing volleyball in the swimming pool or challenging your colleague to a football match?

"Here is a sneak peek into life at EA Romania: fresh fruit every day, excellent medical coverage, travel opportunities to EA offices around the world, multinational teams, and having fun on our EA basketball team! Local facilities include a number of cinemas, shops – but also bars and restaurants for those wanting to enjoy a quick beer after work!"

It's a heart-warming and reassuring bit of detail that doesn't cost anything to offer up but, in many cases, would be swept under the carpet by stuffy corporate bods. Would-be employees can't be difficult to woo.

EA's Global Publishing division is in Geneva, Switzerland, where staff work on marketing, sales, distribution and logistics for games in Europe, Asia-Pacific, Africa and Latin America. It's here that the company's marketing campaigns are drawn up.

Globally, EA has a series of locations and bases: including seven in the US, three in Canada, six in Asia and one in Australia, with a network extending across 12 different countries.

Burnaby, though, is where the main work on the game itself takes place – with slews of artists, designers, engineers and producers using cutting edge technology to produce a world class product every year. In Chapter 6, we explore how…

USA forward Sydney Leroux is motion captured – this summer, she became a World Champion.

6. EA Sports. It's in the game – but how exactly? And who decides?

How the world's greatest game is played out behind the scenes

Creating *FIFA* is a process as fluid as the attacks that gamers play out on screen. While the first release in the series was put together by barely ten people, the current iterations have a comparatively vast team dedicated to them – in all several hundred people work on each *FIFA* game.

That's because the games now have so many different elements to them. And that means EA staff doing lots of different things; from maintaining the servers that host hundreds of thousands of online matches every day, to visiting football clubs with head-scanning technology to improve player likenesses each year.

Whereas, once upon a time, creating a *FIFA* game was something that could be signed off after a few months (with the project complete once the finished product had shipped) nowadays the process is ongoing – the *FIFA* world operates on a 24/7 basis. So much so, that releases often overlap, with staff working on a previous edition right up to the release of its successor, and often beyond. Some elements of gameplay can even take several years to emerge, meaning that development teams can effectively be spread across three or four different titles at any one time.

Nick Channon, Senior Producer of the game, gave an insight into how each new release emerges. He said: "A huge amount goes into creating a new FIFA each year, and there's different layers to it as well – obviously we make the game every year, but we don't necessarily work just on that. For example, the goalkeeper that we introduced in FIFA 15 had been worked on for multiple years before that came in, and the Player Impact Engine – the physics system of FIFA 12 – had been worked on for a number of years before we did that.

"So we're always looking at different technologies that we can bring in. Depending on how they're progressing, we decide when to introduce them. The process year-on-year is listening to feedback based on last year's game, and what people are saying, but you also have to listen over time.

"This year, from FIFA 15, the key things were that it was hard to defend against Bale and Messi, the defensive AI didn't feel like it was working with you all the time, or covering you very well, so that very much influenced what we did for FIFA 16.

"But we also have a number of things that we want to do, we have technologies we are looking at, not necessarily every year, but experimenting with, so you look at all those different components, and you start to bring a feature set together. It's a pretty involved process, but the heart of it will always be player feedback.

"We literally start the day we finish, we never stop – we're coming towards the end of FIFA 16 now and people are starting to think about the future, and things will come up as we finish, so they get put on the list.

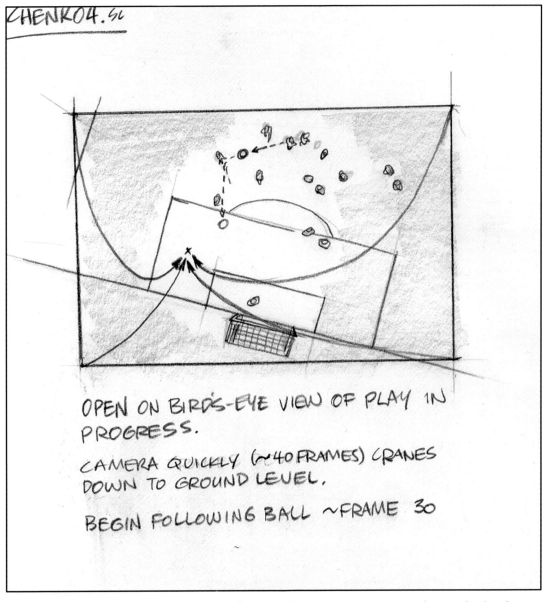

A sketch from the planning of *FIFA 02* – things have progressed massively since.

"So we start with wanting to do X, but we couldn't do that in a year, so we'll think about that longer-term; but Y is great, that's developing something we have; this element is pretty innovative, can we do it, and it's not too involved, so let's bring that in.

You're thinking about one: what the most important things are; and two: how quickly you can do them well.

"We want to make the most authentic, fun experience we can. We won't put something in the game that's authentic if it doesn't make a fun video game. We'll always drive to make the best game that we can. We haven't run out of ideas, every year we're inspired. There's always new inspiration, new technology, there's new ways people are interacting with the game – it's more online and social, what can we do with things like that? The space is always changing so much, so for us it is about keeping up with that."

One major digital focus for *FIFA* is *Ultimate Team*, the game's most popular mode, which is almost wholly online. This means that the FUT team are constantly on the go, often dispersed into different groups to juggle the various components.

The redesign of Ultimate Team cards for *FIFA 16* generated much interest.

For the team's Creative Director, Adam Shaikh, it is something he expects to become the norm for most games and game modes, describing games as transforming into 'online services'. He said: "Everything now is going down the games as a service route. Increasingly, one of the most important things is ongoing work. In the old days, you'd make a disc, put it on the shelf, and then you could wash your hands and do something else.

"Now, there's so much stuff we're doing all the way through the year, there's always new things happening. It's much more blurred. Even fairly recently, we were still doing things for FIFA 15, to improve the experience."

EA Sports' Vancouver studio, which we visited in *Chapter 5*, is testament to this – a hubbub of activity all year round. When I visited, *FIFA 16* was all but completed, but you could easily believe that a project was actually in its infancy, given the pace and intensity of the workers' activity.

As an outsider, it can feel like a daunting place to walk into, but the team in Burnaby are more than receptive to outside influences – especially in the early days of the series, when EA twice flew out a perhaps surprising guest speaker to pass his wisdom onto the staff, commentary legend John Motson.

The affable icon revealed: "Because EA were so conscious that they didn't have the background in soccer as such, they twice flew me across to Vancouver, where they make the game, to do talks and seminars to give them information about what the pitch should look like, to explain the ethos of the game.

"They picked my brains an awful lot in the early years. Obviously, they had the computer skills – that goes without saying – but they didn't have the nuanced knowledge of how we do a football match.

"It was a great experience for me because I'm a complete philistine, I had no idea what the complexities were, or the logistics, until I went to Burnaby. And hopefully I helped them with the football side of things."

If it's something of a shock that Motson was grilled about basics of the game – and that he was diligently quizzed on the aesthetics, too – he has another revelation up his sleeve when it comes to how his commentary recordings were worked in the early years.

He said: "For the first few years, they wrote all the phrases out and I just read them, while on the names I'd do a few different intonations for excited and not-excited and so on. It was very repetitive and demanding – I did it for six hours a day for four consecutive days and that's how we made the game. Just sat in front of a microphone, in a studio in Soho called the Aquarium, and all recordings were whizzed off to Canada for them to add into the game.

"After about seven years, I was in Burnaby one day and I said 'can't we try doing this as though it were a proper football match with me commentating like I normally would?' They thought the game would be too fast for me to cope with, but let me try. And, I'm not trying to be immodest here, but they were bewildered by how I did it – so from then on, they got a co-commentator in, and we did it like that.

"It was like we were working on a live game, with him coming in with summaries and explanations and reactions to incidents. The biggest hurdle was that we couldn't say it was Ryan Giggs, say, because we didn't know which team was going to be playing when they pressed the button.

"The first year I did it, they only really wanted the top European clubs. Then it suddenly went global and we were doing Korean teams and Chinese teams. By the time I left the game, it was worldwide. It certainly moved on from what I would call a very primitive start. The growth of the game has been staggering, absolutely amazing."

Now, it's an all-singing and all-dancing process, that was fine-tuned by Motty and his various co-commentators over the years – including Andy Gray and Alan Smith – with the veteran's berth now filled by *Sky Sports* favourite Martin Tyler.

The broadcast team – made up of four to five artists, six engineers and three producers – focus on creating a virtual version of real world live match coverage. Producer Santiago Jaramillo explains: "When you see the game on screen, you want to be fooled that it's an actual match you're watching on TV. Our job is to blur the line between being on the pitch, in the stadium, and watching on TV. It's almost a seamless blend between those experiences.

"And no matter how amazing the crowd sounds or the players look or the gameplay feels, if it still has a generically branded scoreboard, it takes you out of that feeling. It would be not quite right. If you remember even two years ago, when you were watching the intro to any game, we'd show the line ups but there was no commentary, or it was just generic.

"This year I went to London probably five or six times to work with Martin Tyler and Alan Smith for our commentary recordings. We do multiple days on each trip. Part of the challenge is trying to fit around their schedules, with their Sky contracts and travelling between games – it's difficult to find three or four days in a row. And Martin has to save his voice for the high-intensity things.

"I always imagined you're going to go to this super fancy, high-tech studio, but the one in London is what sounds right – we've been using it for several years and, when you add a bunch of commentary for one year, you want it to stitch together, it should sound like it's all live. So it doesn't look as sexy as you might think, but it works.

"I go there, with an audio artist from my team who can pick out a lot of the subtleties and flag technical issues, with a bunch of scripts, which are usually just guidelines. They improvise most of it.

"I just have to manage the feeling in the room. It's kind of like throwing a party and your job is to make sure everything is right – the lighting is right, the mood is right, the music is right, the food is right – so that the talent performs to the best of their ability.

"They realise the reach of FIFA – Martin always tells me stories about how, when he's walking around London, a lot of the people that stop him recognise him more for his voice in FIFA than for Sky Sports."

Sound is clearly a big focus for *FIFA* – after all, it was the realistic crowd noises that were amongst the most impressive features in the first release – *FIFA International Soccer* – and that's a priority that has remained for EA Sports.

Jaramillo revealed: "We have a great partnership with the Premier League, not just with the overlay and the slick presentation element, but with the crowd recordings. Even if you played FIFA 14, you would notice that the crowd doesn't sound nearly as authentic or immersive – their chants, the reactions – it was a lot more generic, and the quality was a narrow channelling of sound as opposed to the surround sound we have now.

"All that comes from trying to put all these experiences of what it's like to go to a football game, or to watch it on TV, and put them in the game. Sky have been great giving us tons of really high fidelity recordings that we can put in the game. It used to be, many years ago, that they'd get a bunch of guys in a room and they'd fake a chant, but now it's authentic.

"Now we have a 5.1 surround experience with the different channels – you can hear the away crowd over here and you're surrounded by the home crowd's chants. If there are chants that happen in a particular game, we can put that into FIFA, and that's what you hear."

*

Sticking to an aural theme, one of the most important – and probably unexpected – elements of *FIFA* now is its playlist, which has its own dedicated team, who curate a playlist that can make careers. The game has been credited with 'breaking' various stars on a global scale and now commands such status that featuring on the playlist is a highly sought-after spot for up-and-coming bands.

That reputation is a huge, and perhaps surprising, side effect of the series' development – except, of course, to EA, who had exactly such progress in mind. Steve Schnur, now the Worldwide Executive of Music, was the man they turned to, to oversee the brand's first steps in music, having worked for industry giants such as EMI and BMG.

He said: "When I was brought in I was told that we were in an industry, video games, that was bigger than movies, with a once-in-a-blue-moon license, in FIFA. But with mostly Tinker Toy, Casio-created soundscapes. It didn't sound like an enormous industry to me.

"The decision we made was to *not* mimic the live experience – it would have been really easy to put Queen on the video game and then call it in and go home. But, because of the enormity of the medium, we wanted to create a unique sound for it, the sound of the year ahead – as the titles have the next year in them. In the case of football, there's the typical sound, but we wanted to affect what the broadcasters would play, what would be played in stadiums. We wanted the sport to eventually sound like the game, rather than the game sounding like the sport.

"How could we become a complete entertainment medium? I was like a kid in a candy store – I probably wouldn't have taken the gig otherwise, I wasn't here just to license a Gary Glitter song. I wanted to turn people on to something that could dominate, musically speaking, their lives going forward. What a great opportunity – we wanted to be what radio used to be and what MTV used to be."

And it didn't take long for the playlist Schnur curated to start being adopted by radio stations across the world, as his first *FIFA* release, *FIFA Football 2003*, created a huge overnight sensation – Canadian teen singer-songwriter Avril Lavigne, whose breakthrough hit *Complicated* topped charts around the world. Lavigne had been spotted early by Schnur.

"Her first gig ever was in the cafeteria of EAC in Vancouver. I fell in love with this girl who had this pop-punk song that I thought would just sound bad-ass to be used in a sports environment. We had her play at lunchtime for anybody who would come down from the offices to hear this artist they'd never heard before. Then, six months later, they were hearing her on the radio.

"I don't come from games or sports, I come from music – and I still get, even after all these years, goosebumps when an artist all of a sudden moves from twenty people to 20,000 at a gig. An artist that you know you've helped.

"Hopefully, every time we're there early because we know the impact of the placement. It's one of those great fulfilling moments that money can't buy, and we've been through it quite a few times with FIFA.

"FIFA Football 2004 was Kings of Leon; that was their placement. They were a band that had not made any impact in the US. Ironically, I saw them in the UK – I live half the time in Nashville and here was a band from Nashville in the UK. And we just decided to break this band, to put them in FIFA and help introduce them to the world.

"There were other bands, too, like Radiohead, obviously incredibly well known, but they were fairly unlicensable. But we got them on the 2004 playlist because the placement on FIFA meant so much to them."

Landing the English band was a genuine coup, but demonstrated the instant gravitas EA Trax had earned. After appearing on just one iteration of the series, it already had enough of a pull to secure a deal for premium bands.

Schnur, though, is gracious about the impact of his work, downplaying the suggestion that he and his team single-handedly make anyone's career – rather, they are providing them with a platform to launch themselves from… *FIFA*.

"The truth is we approach it the same way now as we did then, we still go with our gut, and imagine where that artist can be on a world stage. We don't want artists that we feel will continue to live in a bubble, as we're about to put them on one of the biggest platforms on the planet.

"We only gave Avril and Kings of Leon an initial platform, but it was a global platform – and they were the ones that lived up to it. We don't listen to the radio and become influenced by other sources. Because, if we did, any band on FIFA would be old by the time the game comes out. We want to influence radio, the broadcast of sports, what's played in stadiums, and an artist's career."

For many players of the game now, EA Trax is effectively their Spotify – the playlist of songs they'll hear more than most others for the coming year. Whether they realised it or not at the start of the mode's introduction, EA proved trendsetters in yet another category – music streaming – with products like Spotify, and subsequently Apple Music and Jay-Z's Tidal, now par for the course. Certainly, those companies aren't considered rivals.

Schnur says: "We've been doing EA Trax for almost 15 years, starting before Spotify was born and there was no such thing as streaming services on a global scale. When we started in 2001, it was a time when records sold a lot, millions of millions copies – the one thing we chose to do back then was to curate, and to find artists.

"MTV stopped playing music for the most part, radio became consolidated and confined, so we decided to live up to what the previous decades had done – to be a place to discover something you may not be able to discover somewhere else.

"We're tethered to a product so we don't have the ability, like Spotify, to offer you millions of songs, so we curate the heck out of the playlist each year. I can't please everybody with every song on the game, but if we can get you with a couple of them – and you can look back and say 'my god, that was the greatest song I remember from 2005' – I think we're doing our job."

Now, with a spot on the EA Trax listings so prized, the process for putting together each year's playlist is a strenuous one, with the self-applied pressure on for Schnur to identify a range of songs suitable for the global brand. And his small team don't just work on *FIFA*; they work across all of EA's titles, from *NHL* to *Battlefield*.

"It's a small team: there's myself, there's a music supervisor, I have a music marketing coordinator, and I have a licensing person. And, give or take, that's pretty much the largest it's ever been. We also work on every other EA game – the orchestrations of Star Wars, the scores for Dragon Age, and the music for Madden.

"When it comes to FIFA, you can't do it just in the US for obvious reasons. You have to know what's going on not just in the UK but in Brazil and Asia, in Italy and so on. You really have to start taking a look at bands in any way, shape or form that you can. Looking at what trends are going online, go to gigs as often as humanly possible – but, because it's a global title, you can't necessarily go out every night and see those bands. So we have to follow from afar – not that they know that we're following them.

"There's the same intention, discovery of music, for FIFA and Madden. But the difference between them, which makes FIFA really appealing, is that it's truly global. FIFA's the only one where we take a look at it from a truly, deeply global perspective. It makes it slightly more challenging.

"I'm sure I'm not even aware of some of the songs from Brazil that we missed. Right from the start, we used to put little flags next to the songs, because we wanted to put out the worldwide perspective, so gamers can feel the global experience.

"Literally the day after a game comes out, we start working on the next year. We're just finishing FIFA 16 this week, and this Fall we'll start working on next year's game. We'll start getting our hands really dirty in about January, but we'll spend the next couple of months starting to survey what's going on out there, and figuring out what bands we might like. Then, in January, there's no turning back.

"By then, we have a shortlist of bands – by June, we have a massive list. We don't eliminate, we add to the list – we only cut it down towards the ends, when we only have so much space and money to license with."

Naturally, sometimes, bands that don't make the list turn out to be a success anyway, which stings the proud Schnur, who admits: "There have been some artists that we've missed and kicked ourselves really hard in the ass after. Once in a while, a band will play us something they haven't recorded yet, and we'll fall in love with it, but they don't finish it in time."

*

One of the most intriguing elements about *FIFA* is the motion capture software adopted to accurately capture real stars' inimitable styles of running, moving and striking of the ball. Maybe it's the curious-looking outfits the technology requires, or just the remarkable results. Either way, MoCap, as the cool kids refer to it, is a crucial part of *FIFA*'s polished end product.

Once the team get a leading athlete into the studio, they then have to take them through a scene-by-scene running order – the sporting star suddenly playing the role of actor, as the producers overseeing the action produce storyboard-style wishlists of moves to recreate. Particularly arduous requests – imagine some of the elaborate and acrobatic trickshots from the *FIFA Street* spin-off series – can require various takes.

For *FIFA 16*, Lionel Messi was charged with demonstrating 'no touch dribbling' for a new feature dreamt up by the EA Sports team. The Argentine's interpretation of that would have been monitored and followed by the 130 or so cameras set up, capturing his movements from every angle possible – their calibrations and settings fine-tuned every morning.

But the lenses aren't focussed on Messi's expression, the colour of his boots, or the way his hair bounces as he moves – instead, they're tracking the reflections of the white spots, known as markers, that are placed variously over his all-black outfit. Skill-aside, it could be anyone taking centre stage – the cameras don't follow the world's leading footballer, just that collection of spots moving in space.

It's when this data is fed into a computer that it starts to take a more human form. Matched with Messi's carefully sculpted in-game character, suddenly *FIFA* has a realistic looking player with authentic movement. Obviously, not everyone will get the Messi treatment – they'll generally capture players of various archetypal body forms, to then be applied to similarly built counterparts. The studio loads various 'buckets' of animation into the EA system, from which the gameplay teams will create the desired physics for the next game.

Such is the reliance on this software that EA built a separate building at the Burnaby campus in 2005, housing a new studio with parallel stages, dressing rooms, a construction workshop, storage and an office. As motion capture is a key element of *FIFA*, the team that works on it is a prominent part of EA Sports.

Nigel Nunn, who is based at the MoCap studio when he isn't touring the footballing world carrying out headscans of players for next year's game, puts the role of the impressive facility into perspective.

He said: "We have a massive space now, it's about 130ft long by about 50ft wide. It used to be a bit smaller, but FIFA actually pushed it because they need to get full runs off the athletes. When sprinting, 50ft was just not long enough for them, they'd only be getting a few strides in, when in full flow.

"The studio is one of the largest in the world now – the US army have a bigger one, technically, because it is taller for rappelling and stuff.

Edgar Davids works as an early MoCap model for *FIFA 01*.

"We have the balls on specific parts, the joints, parts that move, and a red light bounces off the balls and goes back into the cameras – so the camera only sees those reflections. It's kind of like GPS, it tracks the movement, and watches how players move. It's like connect the dots, you just see all these markers, and someone goes in and turns it into a stick man moving about – we use that to drive the 3D model of that person."

Much of the work the team in Vancouver do for the game is carried out with actors – as getting the likes of Messi to Canada for motion capture is an expensive and irregular occurrence. That doesn't mean everything isn't done to the highest level of detail possible, though.

"We've just developed a body scanning system, which is the same as the facescanning one, but which uses 152 cameras – FIFA's been using it to get the wrinkles in jerseys. So we get actors wearing the different kits and doing certain motions to track the way the kit moves.

"And celebrations is another obvious one where we'll pull up YouTube, and get an actor to mimic it in the MoCap Studio after watching it a few times."

Finally, with an eye to the future, Nigel explains: "Messi has a very distinctive running style, but we wouldn't get every single player's individual run captured. Yet."

Another famous visitor to EA's Motion Capture studio.

With the striking realism offered by the game's graphics, and players easily recognisable in pixel form, *FIFA* is justifiably renowned for its high quality visuals. This is something that relies heavily on their attention to detail, which borders on almost obsessional.

The technology behind distinctive and distinguishable players in-game is known as headscanning, with twenty cameras set up in a semi-circle shaped cage, capturing players from virtually every angle. This kit is taken to every Premier League club ahead of each new *FIFA* release, as well as various European sides – and the 12 women's national teams added to *FIFA 16*.

The man in charge of this lengthy process is the aforementioned Nigel Nunn, a Cannuck who lugs the various bits of equipment around the globe, in and out of the world's biggest football clubs – and some of the smaller outfits, too – to meet EA's demands for realism. In all, the kit takes up ten large suitcase-like boxes. Being the company's headscanning specialist doesn't allow for travelling light. In the summer of 2015, he was based in the UK for three months.

Nigel said: "Headscanning came about because we started doing some facial motion capture and then realised we'd need the geometry of the face to go with the animation that we'd captured. Before that we had something called Projected Light and it was really expensive and it took like half an hour. The quality was terrible and you didn't get any of the skin texture, just the shape of the face. We did that on a couple of players – Ronaldinho and Sergio Ramos – at an event in Spain, but it wasn't great.

"So we started using this system, photogrammetry, about seven years ago, where you take photos and the software analyses them to get the shape of the face. So this means you can shoot it in like a second and get the same result that was taking 35 minutes.

Cristiano Ronaldo is added to *FIFA 16*

"When they found out, the FIFA team were like 'oh my god, we can scan everybody in the game' and I was like 'you're so funny', but they were serious – so every year we get about 500 players scanned like this. I travel around, sometimes with a colleague, to slowly chip away at the list. This year was pretty heavy, but in the past I've had to fly back and forth from Vancouver to do two French clubs here, then some English clubs there, and so on.

"Back when we started, we had eight cameras and would rotate the guy around. We didn't take nearly as many pictures and the whole system was really unstable. Now, we do five main shots, captured from each of the different cameras. We start with a neutral, no expression pose, which is the main face scan – the important one from which we'll make 90% of the face.

"Then we take one with their eyes closed and mouth open to get the eye lids; third is eyes really wide so we can see their pupils; the fourth we get them to show us their teeth to get that texture; then we do one of the back of their head; and finally one of the top of their head too, which is really awkward as the player has to stand and bend over for the camera to see it."

Bournemouth's Sylvain Distin undergoes the head-scanning process.
Picture credit: National Football Museum.

Nigel continued: "All told, the whole process takes about ten minutes, then after that we video the players mimicking a woman doing different expressions. We use that to get HD

The numerical breakdown of EA's headscanning technology

We just explored FIFA's headscanning process where players are captured from various angles so that they are recreated as realistically as possible in the game.

To convey the depth and extent of that process, we crunch the numbers involved as Nigel Nunn travels around the footballing world to capture the game's top players.

3,500 The average number of individual images taken per club visit – that means, for the Premier League alone, Nigel has 70,000 different pictures on his hard drive. Talk about a mega-fan.

120 The minimum number of images taken per player – with 20 cameras capturing at least six required poses. This number increases when more references are needed… for long or plentiful hair, for instance.

100GB With each image taking up around 25MB of space – which is super high resolution – a full day of shooting can take up close to 100GB. For those who aren't sure how much that is – it's, roughly, a lot.

40 hours The amount of time it takes, in initial rendering, to turn photos for a squad of 20 players into 3D geometry. The equivalent of a full working week, for a one-man team. After that, there are still a few days of work by a technical artist to get them ready for animation, before they can be put into the game.

Introducing the songs you'll be hearing A LOT of this year

Given the exclusivity of the *FIFA* playlist – with Steve Schnur and his team curating on a best-of-the-best-only basis – it's hard not to have high expectations for the tracks that have made the cut.

So which elite songs will soon be blaring out of your television, causing you to hum sub-consciously between matches? Which songs will you somehow know the words to when you catch them on the radio or whilst out and about?

As you'd probably expect, it's a delicate mix of stellar superstars (see Grammy Award winning singer-songwriters Beck and Sam Smith), trendy acts that are fairly well known but ready for a global push (like Brit singer John Newman), and complete unknowns for anyone outside their home territory (Brazil's Baiana System, for instance).

The 42 tracks are sourced from a wide selection of nations, from Austria to Colombia via New Zealand and Malawi. The UK is the best-represented region, but mostly by unknown underground acts.

So, here is the full rundown of the *FIFA 16* playlist – a set of songs all bidding to enjoy their breakthrough moment. As one of the selections puts it: "One Great Song And I Could Change The World". Quite right.

BAND	SONG	Territory
All Tvvins	Darkest Ocean	IRE
April Towers	A Little Bit Of Fear	UK
Atlas Genius	Stockholm	AUS
AURORA	Conqueror	NOR
Baiana System	Playsom	BRAZ
Baio	Sister Of Pearl	USA
BANNERS	Shine A Light	UK
Bastille	Hangin'	UK
Beck	Dreams	USA
Bomba Estereo	Soy Yo	COL
BØRNS	Fool	USA

BAND	SONG	Territory
Coasts	Tonight	UK
Disclosure	Omen feat. Sam Smith	UK
Durante	Slow Burn feat. Chuck Ellis	IT/USA
Everything Everything	Distant Past	UK
Foals	Mountain At My Gates	UK
Gin Wigmore	New Rush	NZ
Icona Pop	Emergency	SWE
Jax Jones	Yeah Yeah Yeah	UK
John Newman	Tiring Game feat. Charlie Wilson	UK
Kaleo	Way Down We Go	ICE
Kygo	ID	NOR
Louis The Child	It's Strange feat. K. Flay	USA
Miami Horror	All It Ever Was	AUS
No Wyld	Let Me Know	NZ
Nothing But Thieves	Trip Switch	UK
Of Monsters And Men	Crystals	ICE
Parade Of Lights	Feeling Electric	USA
RAC	Back Of The Car feat. Nate Henricks	USA
Raury	Crystal Express	USA
Seinabo Sey	Pretend	SWE
Skylar Grey feat. X Ambassadors	Cannonball	USA
Slaptop	Walls	USA
Speelburg	Lay It Right	UK
Swim Deep	One Great Song And I Could Change The World	UK
The Royal Concept	Smile	SWE
The Very Best	Makes A King feat. Jutty Taylor	Malawi/UK
Tiggs Da Author	Run	UK
Unknown Mortal Orchestra	Can't Keep Checking My Phone	USA
X-Wife	Movin' Up	POR
Years & Years	Gold (FIFA Edit)	UK
Zibra	Goodbye Mondays	UK

The best quips, slips and titbits from the various voices of FIFA

With the pool of commentary phrases expanding every year; in theory we should hear brand new quips and statements from Martin Tyler and Alan Smith. But, of course, that's not the case – and some phrases have become a part of *FIFA* folklore for their regular occurrences (so much so that you could play 'commentary bingo' with them) or just bizarre nature. Here are some of our favourites of both, that we (kinda) hope crop up in *FIFA 16*, too.

"Tevez, with his bulldog-like approach."

Though the powerful forward has left Europe to return to his homeland with Boca Juniors, we're sure this classic line will remain.

"Strong tackle, Bacary Sagna."

Every. Single. Time. It was enough to make gamers avoid the left flank so they did not have to hear the phrase again.

"That was like Alan Smith in his prime, except it isn't in the back of the net."

A bit of a love-in in the *FIFA* commentary box, as Martin Tyler praises his co-commentator – a bit too often for our liking.

"This is Neymar."

Was Tyler secretly working on a football-themed remake of This Is Sparta? If so, his brand awareness must be sky high.

"The bench is concerned, as the player looks to be in severe pain at the moment… but he's a tough lad, I think he'll be able to carry on."

Touchline insight from Geoff Shreeves who, apparently, doesn't have a clue on most injuries in *FIFA*. Especially as, by the time he's finished saying this, you've already been forced to sub said player off with a broken ankle.

"Well, that's the first goal of the game – and it's 1-0."

Yeah, cheers for that, Martin. We weren't sure whether this match might have switched to a tennis-style scoring system. But you've cleared things right up.

Martin Tyler: "What did you make of the team's first half display, Andy?"

Andy Gray: "Two words. Can't defend, Martin."

Tyler: "That's three words."

Gray: "Oh, Martin, yeah alright."

Classic 'banter' from Tyler and Gray, the type of which Gray's replacement Alan Smith must strive towards.

"It's a pass, and a pass, and another pass."

And enough to make you want to give the ball away. Yes, keeping the ball, that's my gameplan. Works for Barcelona.

"It's like a video game."

Alan Smith, you sly old fox.

"The heat was on, but he stayed in the kitchen, and came out with the ball."

What? Who keeps their balls in the kitchen? Steady.

"To win the raffle, you have to buy a ticket."

Breaking: to score a goal you must put the ball in the net. This nasty has been around for years, more recently becoming: 'bought a ticket, nearly won the raffle'.

"And the virtual players go down the virtual tunnel – I wonder what happens to them when they get in there?"

A John Motson classic from *FIFA 96*.

"The morning papers describe this as a friendly match. We'll see how friendly it is when the first tackles start flying in."

Clive Tyldesley made us want to stick to non-friendly fixtures.

"And today's match, controlled by Mehmet Yildiraz."

The hardest working referee in the business is our Mehmet. We say that, because he appeared to be the only official working in *FIFA 15* – or, at least, the only one worth mentioning.

"I've had the misfortune of losing a semi."

Alan Smith gets candid with us while trying to commiserate over a cup loss.

"And, like an archaeologist, this keeper's career is in ruins."

We've saved the best till last – another Motty gem.

Sky Sports commentators Martin Tyler and Alan Smith record audio for *FIFA*.

How a 'gimmicky' addition has become a series mainstay

Introduced alongside Ultimate Team in *FIFA 09* – something that has since seen the importance of their arrival overshadowed – user controlled celebrations have become a hugely important element of the series.

The sceptical amongst us – okay, me included, oops – might have dismissed their introduction as a bit of a gimmick but, actually, they added a unique element to online gameplay; there's little more satisfying than snatching a late winner, and performing the robot aftewards.

The original line up of celebrations wasn't vast – by *FIFA 13*, there were 80 different celebrations included in the game – but the original line-up featured Wayne Rooney performing a series of dance moves in the launch announcement.

Which seems as good an excuse as any for a chapter. Right?

Wayne boogie: We toyed with offering this as a print out 'how to dance' guide.

Shame this wasn't demonstrated by Rooney –
it's his best-known celebration.

This move is known as 'the butt slide'.
Does what it says on the tin.

This one's 'the crouch'. Feels like a trick has
been missed here – Peter Crouch.

Night fever: It seems that virtual Rooney is quite the mover.

Air gui-star: Another classic move appears. Do we smell a dancing spinoff?

New celebrations are influenced by the real world – such as
Samuel Eto'o's response to Mourinho in 2014.

Part Three

What The Game
Has Made

From halfway line to (almost) fully online – FIFA's virtual dominance

In 2015, there are very few elements of daily life that don't revolve around the internet. Being connected, for many, is a necessity. So much so that, in 2011, the UN declared that access to the internet was a *human right*. It's used for communication, commerce and even courting. You might even have bought this book online, too.

FIFA permeates modern culture, particularly online. Video highlights of the latest edition's best goals are almost as common as real-world round ups, while the emergence of Vines – seven-second-long clips that can easily be shared on Twitter and Facebook – offers another almost instant way of sharing players' latest in-game exploits, be they impressive or comical. These bite-sized films often go viral, and are picked up by a whole host of news websites – they know that anything *FIFA* related is almost a guarantee of web traffic.

Jack Wilson, the *Daily Star*'s Online Sports News Editor explains: "There's a huge appetite for FIFA-related content, which is something I didn't expect. You'll see many newspaper sites covering seemingly innocuous videos – such as 'hilarious FIFA fail', 'incredible wonder goal', or just 'Famous Player plays FIFA' – and that's because they get hits.

"I wouldn't say they're more popular than transfer rumour stories – because fans are ravenous for those, particularly over the summer – but FIFA stories can be a very good source of hits in quiet spells. Anything to do with FIFA will attract a certain audience to the website.

"The team who run our Tech section, for instance, will turn to FIFA as a fail-safe way of achieving numbers if they're under pressure for quick fixes. That sums up how popular the game is. Simply, FIFA equals hits."

As well as racking up page views, leading to the emergence of various *FIFA*-specific websites, the game has also played its part in helping to establish the latest celebrity phenomenon – famous YouTubers, many of whom have become renowned for their *FIFA* abilities, good or bad.

While popular YouTubers are famous for a variety of things, from make-up tutorials to virtual cookery classes, many of the top stars from the site are gaming related – and a huge portion of the British examples built their fan bases from *FIFA* clips.

Perhaps the biggest star in that field is KSI, real name Olajide 'JJ' Olatunji, whose infectious enthusiasm while commentating on himself playing the game, has almost established him as a household name – going on to appear on various TV shows – such is his profile. He has built an army of over 10 million online subscribers and his clips and skits have been watched close to two billion times. It's not bad for a man who started uploading videos from his bedroom in Watford, while still a teenager.

The now 22-year-old says: "My first experience of YouTube was in 2006, when I uploaded my favourite Family Guy clips, but they all got removed for copyright infringement. I noticed other YouTubers posting FIFA clips, and I thought that I could do that, if not better. Back then, I'd just score goals and show it to other people – you'd just try to score the best goal ever.

"I'd record it on an old-school device called a Dazzle, which would record footage in black and white. Sometimes it'd work and sometimes it wouldn't, so I wouldn't just be worrying about scoring a goal, I'd be hoping my camera was recording too.

"I saw other YouTubers start to add commentary to their videos, and I wanted more engagement, so I did the same. I started to rant about the game's flaws, and that'd do well for me as people would often agree."

As his posts grew in popularity, KSI developed a following, and an unexpected career was in the offing, as *YouTube* pay royalty fees for users attracting a certain number of views. It took an otherwise directionless teenager and gave him a purpose.

KSI reflects: "If it wasn't for YouTube, I'd probably be homeless by now, or depressed in Uni. There was nothing I wanted to do; I didn't know what I wanted to be. It was a blessing that YouTube came. It was just a hobby, then all of a sudden it started to kick off – I was like 'Oh my God, this could be my job', and it's the best job ever.

"When the pay cheques started to come in, at the end of 2011, after about two years of making videos, I realised that YouTube could be my career. My parents didn't get it. They were like 'No, you can't make money from games'; they thought it was a waste of time, that I should go out and get a proper job.

"But a big thing was talking to a teacher, and telling him that I just didn't enjoy school, that I was having way more fun doing YouTube. When I told him I was making around £1,500 a month, he said I was making more than him. That was when I realised I should put more into it. And, eventually, my parents saw that I was committed to it, and that I was making money. Then it blew up."

Suddenly, KSI wasn't just making money, he was making a lot of it, and he was becoming something of a celebrity in his own right. Increasingly, he was being recognised in the street, and able to live the A-list lifestyle.

He says: "The first time I got recognised was at an Arsenal match. I was with my friends, and this guy just came up to me. I couldn't believe someone had recognised me from YouTube. But actual people watch me; it's not just numbers on a screen.

"From then on, it just got more often. It's got to a point now where every time I go out I get recognised. But I don't worry about that. I love dressing like a tramp, especially if I go to a good hotel, where they're extremely snobby. They look at me like there's no way I can afford to be there. They treat me like I'm in the wrong place. Then I book a sick room and they can't believe it.

"I hate the word 'celebrity' because it suggests I'm somewhat above people, but I'm not – it's just that a lot of people watch my videos. When they meet you, some people cry, a lot of people shake, they get so nervous. It doesn't make sense for me. It's surreal.

"The neighbours know we're famous now. We get quite a few fans coming to the house. They usually see my car (a sports car with a personalised number plate on) and knock. We tried to pretend we didn't live here, but eventually, people put two and two together from what they'd seen on YouTube or Instagram.

"I've worked with so many footballers, like Rio (Ferdinand) and The Ox (Alex Oxlade-Chamberlain). I'm able to contact quite a few famous people at any time I want – if I want to do a video with them – people you wouldn't normally be able to contact. I'm able to Direct Message Floyd Mayweather on Twitter, for instance. He followed me first!"

YouTube **sensation KSI relaxes at home. Photo courtesy of Jim Bennett.**

Inspired by KSI and his counterparts, teenage boys are now as likely to say they want to be a YouTuber when they grow up as they are to answer 'footballer', with similar rewards seemingly on offer. Though KSI dispels any suggestion that it's easy money being a *YouTube* sensation: "Lots of people say YouTube is easy, anyone can do it, but when they try, they realise it's hard work. There's so much you need to think about. Recording a video is the easy bit, that's just playing, that takes maybe an hour – but the editing process takes hours. On a typical day, I wake up around 2pm, I go straight into edit mode from the recording I've done the night before.

"I'll check a few Vines, see what's trending and try to implement that into my videos. I'd be done around 8pm, then I'd record some more videos for my channels, and then again as a group, and then edit until 6am. Sometimes, if I work hard enough, I'll get a free day, when I'll do something just to get out of the house."

And KSI isn't the only personality who has established a profile as a result of *FIFA* videos – there's a whole squad-full of them. Literally, as phone giants EE discovered in a publicity campaign over the summer of 2015. Rather than sign up various reality television stars or trendy pop artists, the company recruited 27 of the world's most popular *FIFA* YouTubers, to face off in a real-world match at Wembley, the day after the FA Cup final.

Footage was captured during the build-up to the clash and in the match itself, and then made into a ten-episode series published on EE's *YouTube* account. With more than 27 million subscribers between them, the *YouTube* stars were considered a sure-fire way to generate traffic for EE, who also forked out for former England players Ray Wilkins and Martin Keown to be guest managers of the two sides.

In the project overview document, put together by EE's PR team, they explain the choice of *YouTube* stars rather than 'normal' celebrities, pointing to their established fan bases "that reach internationally, including the US".

Similarly popular on *YouTube* is the official EA Sports *FIFA* channel, which has 1.6 million subscribers, racking up more than 300 million video views, The thirst for *FIFA* footage is almost insatiable.

*

It's not just YouTubers that are playing *FIFA* online. Millions around the world take on friends and strangers over the internet, too. On an average day, millions of *FIFA* matches take place online. In the Ultimate Team mode, alone, there are more than three million games played daily.

And that has bred a whole new area of sport, known as eSport, which is basically a jazzy, modern name for competitive gaming. But put those geeky stereotypes to the back of your head – if only briefly – as eSports are positively mainstream. So much so that millions watch online, special tournament events sell out football stadiums from America to Korea via Germany, and leading bookmaker Paddy Power even takes bets on the outcome. It's a whole other world.

Emmett Murphy, B2B Sports Risk Manager at *Paddy Power* says: "The biggest eSports games played are Dota 2 (Defence of the Ancients), LOL (League of Legends) and StarCraft II.

"In August 2015, we offered betting on The International 2015, a tournament that had an $18million prize, making it the largest single tournament to date. The e-gaming sector is growing and, in the future, we hope to expand the offering further with more markets per event, while BIR (live betting) is also a realistic possibility.

"eSports in 2014 saw a global prize pool of $36million, with some 71 million viewers tuning in to watch games in 2013. As an industry, it is expected to grow to $465million by 2017. The arrival of dedicated e-gaming betting websites across the internet demonstrates the market's growing popularity."

Mainstream attention has come thick and fast for the rapidly growing market with outlets such as *Vice Magazine* covering the latest from the competitive gaming world alongside updates for football, tennis and Formula 1. And there's plenty to report on – from the *Pokemon* World Championships, hosted in Boston in 2015, to the titans of *Call of Duty* gaming slugging it out at the X Games, where the first video game event was held at the annual extreme sports event, alongside snowboarding, surfing and motocross.

Similarly, *Red Bull* – rarely a company to invest in a sport after the curve – has made forays into eSports, with the suggestion being that they could soon emerge as the highest profile eSports team on the planet.

With that in mind, EA Sports made another savvy brand move, creating the *FIFA Interactive World Cup* (*FIWC*) to crown the best player on the planet. Starting in 2004, in Switzerland, the finals tournament has developed into a gala event, with the 20 finalists participating in a showpiece knockout tournament for the crown, broadcast across the globe to more than a million viewers. It is now officially recognised by *Guinness World Records* as the world's largest online gaming tournament and has hosted events around the world – from England to the US, Brazil to the UAE.

In attendance at each 'Grand Final' is a dedicated commentary team, renowned in the eSports arena; plus presenters Kay Murray, of *beINsports USA* and Alan McInally, a *Sky Sports* pundit. There are also various celebrity guests. At the 2015 event in Munich, it was real-world World Cup winner Christoph Kramer and Bayern Munich star David Alaba. Before the final match, singer Kwabs performed a three-song set in the auditorium where the match took place.

2015 *FIWC* champion Abdulaziz Alshehri poses with Bayern defender David Alaba.

An approximate 1.2 million people entered the 2015 tournament's qualification process online, before national shoot-outs took place in person, qualifying players for the finals. Current champion Abdulaziz Alshehri, from Saudi Arabia, earned a cheque for around £13,000 when lifting the title and two tickets to the next Ballon d'Or event, where he will brush shoulders with the world's elite players of the real game.

That makes it the most lucrative football gaming tournament in a young but expanding genre. Elsewhere, Gfinity put on the Play Like a Legend tournament in 2015, the first to focus on Ultimate Team, which rewarded winner EmiBoost34 with a cheque for $5,000. *FIFA*'s first steps into eSports have been successful with *FIWC* becoming a recognised global event, earning credibility and a following. In the future, it'll only grow.

French gamer EmiBoost34 with his $5,000 winner's cheque for Play Like a Legend.

Kay Murray, who has been involved with the *FIWC* finals for the last three years, flying in from her base in the US, can vouch for that. She says: "It was something very different from most other event hosting gigs, which was one of the reasons I was quick to accept the role.

"One of the great things about the FIWC Grand Final is that it's not something that's done by half. The magnitude of the event, the host cities and the opportunities the finalists get to experience a bit of culture, away from the gaming, are what makes it even more special.

"Video gaming is becoming like an actual sport. It's shaping up to be a lucrative career path for some, bringing them fame and fortune. Let's face it, who doesn't want to make money doing something they love? The glamour and prestige of the event is also helping it grow, as has the rise of social media – making the tournament qualifiers more accessible."

FIWC presenters Kay Murray and Alan McInally offer analysis of the virtual action.

Though the tournament might sound relatively new-fangled and modern, it can have a life-changing effect on its entrants. For English teenager Chris Bullard, entering the first *FIWC* in 2004, on a whim, would dramatically alter his life plan.

He says: "I got involved just by looking online for competitions, and FIWC was in its first year, so I entered online. I was only 17, and growing up I'd always been the better out of my mates and was pretty good online too.

"That year, the 2004 tournament, I finished in the top 50 in the world, which wasn't enough to qualify for the Grand Final but gave me confidence that I was good enough to. The next year, in 2005, it was hosted in England, and I ended up winning the whole thing.

"It was a rare case of someone turning up and becoming a world champion in their first event. And that changed my life big time: FIFA was my favourite pastime as a kid, but suddenly, I had to take it seriously.

"The year building up to winning FIWC was a big deal, putting the practice in and actually really wanting to achieve something. To do something like that at such a young age was incredible. At that point, I didn't know if I was going to get rich out of doing it, whether I could make a living from it, or what?

"It was really a fun time, travelling the world for free and getting paid money to do it. I gave up a construction apprenticeship to become a gamer full-time, which was a big decision at the age of 20. But I was still young, so I could take that risk, whether it worked out or not.

"My family were great about it, really supportive, though I'd taken my dad to the FIWC finals and the Ballon d'Or gala, so that probably helped. When we were there it was surreal. I met Ronaldinho, Samuel Eto'o and Frank Lampard – who was actually sent off for me in my FIWC final, so it was really funny talking about that. I remember being backstage eating my dinner and Ian Wright coming over to chat and being wowed by me.

Former *FIWC* champion August Rosenmeier takes on German World Cup winner Christoph Kramer.

"I was officially contracted as a pro gamer for two years, but I did it on a self-employed basis for three-and-a-half years – I got enough from tournament winnings to keep going for a little while.

"eSports is so huge now, the massive ones like DOTA and StarCraft have huge cult followings. You see, the generation now coming up – ten years behind me – I knew would be big, because I was at the forefront of that movement. I was 16 when online gaming was created, console-wise."

As well as becoming *FIFA* world champion in 2005, Chris also went on to compete in the World Cyber Games – the South Korean-created event sponsored by *Samsung* and *Microsoft* – on five different occasions. He was also associated with British eSports team *Team Dignitas* for the best part of a decade.

However, for Chris, now 28, it is a world he has since left behind – after completing a degree, he works as a business analyst for an insurance company – but he looks back fondly on his time as a pro gamer, saying: "I was signed to an American TV show, Championship Game Series, which went out on Sky and which gave me an official base salary.

"It wasn't enough money to buy a house or car, or to make me rich, but it was enough to live off as a 20-year-old – to not have to worry about anything other than gaming. It was a great, fun time and something amazing to be able to do while I was young."

Chris Bullard collects his *FIWC* title at the 2005 Ballon d'Or gala.

With burgeoning online popularity comes an expectation and obligation to cultivate and manage a community, something EA were quick to recognise with *FIFA*'s mass appeal. One of the people responsible for that is Rob Hodson, who has been Social and Community Manager on the game for the last three years.

He says: "Community management is becoming par for the course for almost every industry, it seems. It's becoming an evolution of personal service and marketing and everything rolled into one. There's a need for something in the middle, between the customer and the company.

"Our community is getting a lot bigger, the volume has changed dramatically recently. From a convenience perspective, people are almost wanting the same sort of information, the prices, how to trade, how to win games, and so on.

"Probably the biggest change in recent years is the introduction of FUThead and FUTwiz, which are price tracking websites. Prior to that, it was entirely down to someone's knowledge. If you wanted to know the price of a player, you had to follow that yourself and make notes. Then these sites came along and suddenly that process was all automated.

"The FIFA community are extremely passionate. It's safe to say that their footballing passion very much overflows into the game as well. Everything you can take from football, in terms of it being a religion, is very much echoed in the game community as well. There are a lot of games where people are extremely dedicated, but with FIFA the football link exaggerates that. A lot of these guys only play FIFA. They just need football in their life all the time. Other gaming communities have dedicated players, but it's quite likely they're dedicated to other games as well.

"That's something we want to make the most of. We are working with certain active YouTubers in the community and promotion streaming through the likes of Twitch. For example, we did a charity stream with a guy called Castro, which raised more than £50,000 for Macmillan Cancer Support and St. Jude Children's Research Hospital. That sort of thing demonstrates the scope and scale of the community."

As well as those that the game has helped to make famous, *FIFA* can boast some high profile fans – with its role in helping professional footballers socialise and kill time proving invaluable. Not that they're always happy with the game, with particular debate centring on their ratings when each new iteration is announced…

The FIWC Hall of Fame

The gamers who can call themselves a *FIFA* world champion, and a mention for the runners up – well, they deserve something, don't they?

Switzerland 2004	England 2005	Holland 2006	Germany 2008	Spain 2009
Winner: Thiago Carrico de Azevedo (Brazil)	Winner: Chris Bullard (England)	Winner: Andries Smit (Holland)	Winner: Alfonso Ramos (Spain)	Winner: Bruce Grannec (France)
Runner-up: Matija Bilkeskovic (Serbia)	Runner-up Gabor Mokos (Hungary)	Runner-up: Wolfgang Meier (Austria)	Runner-up: Michael Ribeiro (USA)	Runner-up: Ruben Morales Zerecero (Mexico)
Final score: 2-1	Final score: 5-2	Final score: 6-4	Final score: 3-1	Final score: 2-1

FIWC 2012 champ Alfonso Ramos takes on Gerard Pique, cheered on by Lionel Messi.

Spain 2010	USA 2011	UAE 2012	Spain 2013	Brazil 2014	Germany 2015
Winner: Nenad Stojkovic (Serbia)	Winner: Francisco Cruz (Portugal)	Winner: Alfonso Ramos (Spain)	Winner: Bruce Grannec (France)	Winner: August Rosenmeier (Denmark)	Winner: Abdulaziz Alshehri (Saudi Arabia)
Runner-up: Ayhan Altundag (Germany)	Runner-up: Javier Munoz (Colombia)	Runner-up: Bruce Grannec (France)	Runner-up: Andrei Torres Vivero (Mexico)	Runner-up: David Bytheway (England)	Runner-up: Julien Dassonville (France)
Final score: 2-1	Final score: 4-1	Final score: 1-0	Final score: 1-0	Final score: 3-1	Final score: 3-0

**Jurgen Klopp presents 2013 *FIWC* champ
Bruce Grannec with his winner's certificate.**

2014 champ August Rosenmeier gives his top playing tips

With around two million gamers entering the *FIWC* qualifying process each year, the competition to get to a finals event is huge – and every little edge needs to be exploited. So, for a reader of this book, who maybe wasn't aware of the tournament previously, but fancies themselves as a world-beater – what's the best way to get started on the road to inevitable glory?

Thankfully, August Rosenmeier, the 19-year-old former World Champion – as well as three time Nordic champion and two-time Danish champion – from Copenhagen is on hand to offer some pointers.

He, too, had to start from somewhere. Inspired by watching *FIWC 2011*, he became determined to qualify for the next event – which he did – reaching the *FIWC* Grand Finals in Dubai. "That was a great experience for me," he says. "I didn't really go far in the tournament, but it was a big deal to be there and play against the best players in the world."

By the time of the next finals event, in Madrid in 2013, he reached the quarter finals, where he lost to eventual winner Bruce Grannec in the final – finishing as the only man to have beaten the Frenchman, having come out on top during a group stage meeting. It was a heart-breaking way to go out, but the Dane emerged bigger and better as a result.

"The word intense describes it all – the players are so focussed and there's a lot of nerves. Those are the three key words – intense, focussed, and nerves – for the FIWC players. There's so much intensity, you want to win of course, that's why over two million people try to qualify, because the prize is great and that reflects in the nerves – people know what's on the board.

"Rio 2014 was third time lucky for me. That was one of the biggest to win because the real World Cup was held at the same time, and you could definitely feel the spirit. It was a big relief to go all the way.

"After I won, the news were after me, I got a lot of attention back home. My Facebook fan page went from four thousand likes to more than ten, and now I have almost twenty. People recognise me in the street, and I have signed some autographs too since that victory."

Meeting of world champs: Rosenmeier meets Ronaldo.

Now ranked as number two in the *FIFA* world, and something of a *FIWC* veteran after appearing in four straight Grand Finals tournaments, there are few in the world better placed to dish out advice for future challengers.

So, the basics – who shall we play as, and with what formation?

August says: "Tactics-wise, when it comes to formations and teams, it's 4-2-3-1, and the best team is Real Madrid. In 2015, we had to play with national teams, which was a great idea, so people weren't just watching Madrid versus Madrid.

"The strongest countries are Brazil, Portugal, Germany, France and Argentina. These five were the most popular at the FIWC finals. Every country has their profiles – Portugal has Cristiano Ronaldo, Brazil has speed and technique, Germany and France have power and strength, while Argentina has Lionel Messi and Sergio Aguero. Every country and every team has their own strengths, and also of course their weaknesses, but that's just a choice you've got to make."

Okay, so we've avoided picking England, and have gone for a fairly obvious superpower as our team of choice – adopting the trendy 4-2-3-1 formation like the mini-Mourinho that we are – now we can focus on the more technical specifics of *FIFA*. Or, rather, a certain world class Danish *FIFA* star can. Here, August presents his top five tips for virtual footballing success.

1. Always aim to be better by playing against players who are on your level or better than you, and then copy or steal the tricks they use and try to implement them into your game. That's how I came to the top, to be honest. I started to play serious *FIFA* after watching the 2011 FIWC finals on YouTube, and decided I wanted to be there the following year. I was not one of the best at that time, so had to learn from others.
2. Have patience in your build up play. There's no need to rush it. Of course, you can play a direct style, but as long as you have the ball, you are open and can score. That's something that has secured me a lot of titles.
3. Attempt as many tournaments as possible. What people don't know is that there's a huge mental aspect at tournaments, especially at FIWC finals. I wouldn't say there's a lot of difference in the skill level between number one and number twenty, but the

mental aspect is so important. If you can control your nerves, you definitely have an advantage. There's a big difference between sitting on your couch at home and playing online to playing in Rio in front of many people to get $20,000.

4. Use your key player as best as possible. Look at his stats and what he's good at then try to put him in the key moments. If I have Ronaldo, I will always try to find him in the box, because he can win me the game every time. In the FIWC 2015 final, the winner Abdulaziz Alshehri looked for Ronaldo every time, because he's the best player in the game. He converted for him, and literally gave Abdul the title. That's why it's so important to use your players, as they'll make the difference in the hard games.

5. It's important that you look at your centre backs' pace and strength. You need two centre backs who are not slow, it's important that they can at least run. Normally, you will always put your best offensive player in the attack and, if I'm playing against Ronaldo, I really need someone who is capable of running with him during the sprints. They also need strength so they can push Ronaldo away. In general, you need pace and strength on your team. That's what makes the difference on the big stage.

Exclusive company: The best players in the world, virtual and real.

Aside from in-game tactics, stats and playing style, pre-match preparation can also play a part in FIFA.

Just as real life teams will go through training drills to counter specific threats from their opposition, and enjoy certain weekend rituals to make sure they're ready for action, there's work you can do to warm up nicely for your big match – whether that's the *FIWC* final, or just a face-off against the mate you never seem able to defeat.

August offers some insight into his routine, saying: "Before a big game, drink as much water as you can get. It's important to have as much concentration as possible and I always try to drink at least a bottle before a tournament game. With food, I usually just eat some fruit or something healthy.

"Sleeping is also important. Preparing is a big part of competitive FIFA - and you will have better opportunities if you relax and eat well before a tournament."

Footballers play with themselves

If you were a professional footballer, training most days, travelling to and from matches every weekend, surrounded by a group of blokes who predominantly discuss tactics, the last thing you'd think you'd want to do is something related to the sport in your downtime – your few, stolen moments of peace without having to listen to your manager talk in clichéd circles.

Perhaps your hobbies would be reading, learning another language, letting off fireworks in your bathroom, or at least chasing women. However, for many stars, *FIFA* is a major pastime – a way to switch off and escape from their day-to-day lives, while still relating to their one true love, football. West Brom defender, Joleon Lescott, is widely considered to be the strongest English professional footballer when on the virtual field, although his Premier League colleagues are getting increasingly competitive.

Playing *FIFA* serves a crucial role within team harmony, by helping to bring clubmates together, initiating new signings into the squad socially over the summer, and is a key, time-killing cure for those long weeks abroad during an international tournament or pre-season tour.

Wayne Rooney and John Terry famously and controversially spoke out about getting itchy feet during the 2010 World Cup in South Africa, with the England squad on lockdown under Fabio Capello's dictatorial rule – you can be sure there were more than a few *FIFA* nights held on that trip.

In much the same way as card schools – or dentist chairs – once did, *FIFA* sessions offer valuable bonding time for a squad of players, particularly at international level, when players from rival factions domestically come together as a unit. The banter exchange as a result of the game can help break any frostiness between individuals without the need for alcohol (the modern manager's nightmare).

By way of example, when the Brazil national team travelled to South Africa for a fixture in March 2014, some of the squad spent their rest time organising a 12-man *FIFA* tournament. It included captain Thiago Silva, national posterboy Neymar, David Luiz, Marcelo, Oscar, Fernandinho, Julio Cesar, Rafinha, Fred, Jo, Paulinho and Hulk.

They drew four groups of three players, before a knock-out stage. Typically, Neymar emerged as the victor, beating strike partner Fred 1-0 in the final, while powerful winger Hulk finished last. It proved a perfect warm up for the real action – Neymar grabbing a hat-trick as Brazil ran out 5-0 winners over their hosts, with fellow *FIFA* gamers Oscar and Fernandinho also getting on the scoresheet.

According to 2014 *FIWC* world champion August Rosenmeier, taking a trip through the stats of each edition's player pool can unearth some unexpected gems, and potentially change which team you want to use. In *FIFA 16*, for instance, he suggests… West Ham.

He says: "The overall player ratings are actually not that important. Obviously, it'll be better if Cristiano Ronaldo or Zlatan Ibrahimovic is rated higher, if that's the player you want to play with.

"But the most important stats are how strong the player is and how fast he is – the physical element in the game is very important, as in all the previous FIFA versions, so that's what the pro players most likely are looking at.

"If you have a player like Cheikhou Kouyate from West Ham and you look at Thomas Muller from Bayern Munich, of course the overall rating is important there, and Muller's will be higher – but the gap between them isn't that big. Kouyate is also a very good player because of his physics.

"That's what people look at. People will be looking at the top fifty players list to help choose which team they'll play as. Most will go with Ronaldo because of his physics, and how tall he is – which is also very important, because crosses play a big part. Unfortunately, Messi doesn't match up on FIFA – he really doesn't have any strength. Which is why people don't really play with Barcelona so much, because Messi, Andres Iniesta and Neymar are not big enough to defend the ball. That's why teams like Real Madrid, Chelsea and Man City are more popular."

But it's not just the diehard gamers that are caught up in the frenzy of the numbers involved in *FIFA* – incredibly, perhaps, the actual players are equally fascinated by how they're rated by EA's statisticians.

The release of *FIFA 15* proved particularly controversial amongst Premier League players. When asked about his role in the game by an unsuspecting interviewer at an EA event, QPR and former Manchester United player Rio Ferdinand was positively apoplectic about the levels applied to his new team mates, as well as his former colleagues at Old Trafford.

He embarked upon an 11-minute tirade – footage of which is now locked away safely in an EA vault – raging: "You've got to do your research. What's going on? Can you please put the right stats on the Man Utd players and also now I'm at QPR can you elevate their stats to the right level?"

And he added, tongue more in cheek: "I don't know who's doing the stats at headquarters but if you want me to come down there and talk to you properly, face to face, I'll do that."

For brother Anton, playing for Reading at the time of the game's release, there was a more surface-level complaint: "I just hope this year they've got rid of the cornrows. I tweeted at them last year, I think it was about five years ago I had cornrows, so I hope this year they got rid of them."

And even *FIFA 15* cover star Eden Hazard, head and shoulders above his peers as Chelsea's main man, had a quibble with his virtual recreation. He said: "I'm too small. I need to be taller by about three or five centimetres." As diminutive men everywhere will testify in Eden's defence, every inch counts – even when in pixel form. Although, in a more official capacity, the diddy trickster added: "I have played FIFA all my life and it's a huge honour to be asked to be on the cover of FIFA 15. Now I have played the game, I can say it's the most realistic football game I have ever seen."

Perhaps the most diva-ish moan about the game, though, came from Manchester City's famously grumpy Samir Nasri – not adverse to petulance or the odd tantrum, just ask the French national team – who was incredibly picky about the speed rating given to him on the game.

He said: "I'm not quite happy with my speed in the game, especially because I play on the wing. I am quite a bit quicker than I am in the game – I'm only rated 81 or 82 (out of 100). It's not enough." Yeah, that's *real* low, Samir.

Being similarly perfectionist in their approach, EA would have certainly heeded any complaints – but, in the case of the players irritated by stats, the footballers could let their feet do the talking.

That's because, in modern *FIFA*, nothing is fixed – stats fluctuate to reflect and represent form and improving players. Harry Kane, for instance, would not have started *FIFA 15* as one of the game's top forwards, but you can be certain he was amongst them come May after an incredible breakthrough season. Such is the realism of *FIFA*, rapid real-life developments can be mirrored almost immediately.

It can also add fuel to the fire of the Ballon d'Or debate – a two horse race between La Liga's leading lights Cristiano Ronaldo and Lionel Messi. Given that the latter is the *FIFA* cover star, it wouldn't take a huge leap of imagination to conjure a conspiratorial analysis of why he was *FIFA 15*'s best-rated player.

Other points of debate generated by the release of a list of the game's top 50 rated players – a now annual event, usually a few weeks before the game itself is available, to pique interest – included crowning Hazard as the Premier League's top star in tenth place, while the most expensive footballer in history, Gareth Bale, was ranked just 14th. This was despite Bale's pivotal role in Real Madrid's Champions League success the year prior.

At Manchester United, former *FIFA* favourite Rooney fell from favour spectacularly – considered by the 15 iteration of the game as the 23rd best player in the game, the ex-cover star was ranked as just the third best striker at his *club*, behind Robin van Persie (11th) and Falcao (12th), although that was still a place ahead of Manchester City counterpart Sergio Aguero.

Not that *FIFA* made many contentious calls. Demonstrating their foresight, EA Sports ranked Thibaut Courtois three places ahead of then-Chelsea rival Petr Cech, as the young Belgian stopper was about to inherit the Czech's crown.

The top ten players in the world, ahead of the 2014/15 season, according to *FIFA 15* were:

1. Lionel Messi, Barcelona
2. Cristiano Ronaldo, Real Madrid
3. Arjen Robben, Bayern Munich
4. Zlatan Ibrahimovic, Paris Saint-Germain
5. Manuel Neuer, Bayern Munich
6. Andres Iniesta, Barcelona
7. Luis Suarez, Barcelona
8. Bastian Schweinsteiger, Bayern Munich
9. Franck Ribery, Bayern Munich
10. Eden Hazard, Chelsea

*

When they're not het up about whether their sprint speed is accurately depicted in the virtual world or not, footballers can also employ *FIFA* for some real-world use, too. It would be generous to describe it as 'training' but, certainly, a game on their console can help a player's preparation for a big game.

That's because it helps them plan what they intend to do when they step onto the pitch. Most of football's biggest stars have talked about the role of visualisation on the night before a match. Rooney says of his prep schedule: "I always like to picture the game the night before. I'll ask the kit-man what kit we're wearing so I can visualise it. It's something I've always done, from when I was a young boy. It helps to train your mind to situations that might happen the following day.

"I think about it as I'm lying in bed. What will I do if the ball gets crossed in the box this way? What movement will I have to make to get on the end of it? Just different things that might make you one per cent sharper."

Though it's an approach that Rooney is clearly comfortable with, it wouldn't necessarily be ideal for every player – certainly those who are less able to focus. Which is where *FIFA* comes in. Why squint your eyes as you try to imagine your club kit, when you can simply load it up on the game? And, similarly, rather than try to conjure various different crossing scenarios in your head, why not just play a few games of *FIFA* to do that for you? Whether consciously or not, a quick game of *FIFA* can help players go through this visualisation process without putting too much thought into it.

Dortmund defender Mats Hummels alluded to this when discussing the game, saying: "Obviously, a professional footballer can use his own experience to manage certain situations in the (virtual) game. Conversely, some people maybe use what they learn in FIFA when they find themselves on a pitch."

It seemed to work for Parma goalkeeper Marco Ameila, who saved a penalty from AC Milan's Ronaldinho in 2008 – crediting it to his virtual experiences. He said afterwards: "It was just like playing against [Ronaldinho] on PlayStation – he had the same run-up. It was very strange."

But, as the saying goes, fact is often stranger than fiction, and there are some real life occurrences that even *FIFA* can't prepare footballers for, as Scotland international Ikechi Anya discovered when scoring against World Champions, Germany, in September 2014. He exclaimed on Twitter: "I scored past Manuel Neuer. Wow! I can't even do that on FIFA."

And *FIFA* has even generated its own cult figures within the footballing world – latching onto the popularity of burly AFC Wimbledon front man Adebayo Akinfenwa, already notorious for his monstrous frame, EA Sports teamed up with the lower league striker to create social content around the game.

It included making 'The Beast' the strongest player on *FIFA 14* and *FIFA 15*, something he understandably relished, gamely playing up to his new role by demonstrating his ability to bench press 180kg (more than two average men) in viral videos for the game.

Not that he plays as himself – rated 62 overall on the game, versus Messi (93) and Ronaldo (92). He told *The Mirror*: "I like playing FIFA, although not with myself on the game that much, as I'm pretty slow and it's frustrating.

"I try and score a couple of worldies with myself every now and again – as in real life I'm always scoring headers – but that doesn't happen too often. My kids are old enough just to button bash now, but they recognise Daddy is in the game, which is nice and I enjoy that."

*

It won't come as much of a shock to discover that it didn't take EA Sports long to latch onto the celebrity interest in their game. Indeed, officially organised *FIFA* tournaments are pretty common at Premier League clubs these days – with players vying to be club champion and then division champion.

The official EA Sports website offered video footage of a whole host of Pro Player Tournaments, with 17 different events featured, ranging from crowning club champions at Chelsea, Manchester City and Barcelona, to hosting a Liverpool vs Everton *FIFA* grudge match, and joining up with the Germany under-21 squad.

To demonstrate the game's pulling power, the FC Barcelona Pro Player Tournament attracted eight of the Catalans' first teamers – including Messi, Neymar, Dani Alves, Gerard Pique, Jordi Alba and Ivan Rakitic. Filmed behind the scenes at the Camp Nou, after morning training was completed, a four-on-four match was played out – with footage of that seemingly innocuous match-up receiving almost six million views on *YouTube*.

At Man City, Sergio Aguero teamed up with Samir Nasri to take on Yaya Touré and Dedryk Boyata, with Aguero and Nasri coming out on top. Nabil Bentaleb and Andros Townsend saw off Christian Eriksen and Eric Dier for the crown at Tottenham, while Aston Villa's

Lose to Balotelli

What? Even Mad Mario can score against you? If you come off second best to Balo's side, with the Italian striker scoring in open play – we're being fair – then you're treating your mates to a fireworks show…

Concede a Sturridge hat-trick

You know where this one is going – let Daniel Sturridge score three and you have to perform his signature celebration every time your opponent demands so, for the next week. Yes, even in public.

New York, New York: don't lose to this lot unless you're good at accents.

Lose to an MLS side

Beaten by three or more goals by a side from MLS? You're talking in an American accent for the next 24 hours. Unless it's Steven Gerrard's LA Galaxy, in which case you're going Scouse, or Frank Lampard's New York City, which means cockney slang for you.

Let Ashley Young score

What are you, blind? If Manchester United's, erm, 'clumsy' winger gets on the scoresheet in a victory over you, then you've got to perform a very dramatic dive when someone walks past you in the street. It's what he would have wanted.

Allow any player to score five

How does that even happen? No matter who scores those goals, though, you better get liking them – you've got to change your Facebook name to include their surname. Let's hope it isn't Dutch defender Virgil van Dijk.

Fail to beat Cech

If you lose to Arsenal or the Czech Republic, without being able to breach Petr Cech's defences, then you'll need to forget about your fancy hairstyle – you're wearing a goalkeeper helmet for the next 24 hours.

Fail to beat Howard

Lose to Everton or the USA with Tim Howard between the sticks, and you've got to pay up – in tribute to the American keeper, you must grow a beard for at least a month. If you can't grow any facial fuzz, find yourself a fake one.

This is *not* a sight you want to be seeing if you like the cleanly-shaved look.

Lose to Zlatan

Well, it's probably only natural, but you've still got to pay. If the self-professed best player in the world, Zlatan Ibrahimovic, scores against you, consigning you to defeat, you must take to a public setting of your opponent's choice, and scream "I AM ZLATAN!" at the top of your lungs.

Get sent off as Sergio Ramos

The Spanish defender has one of the worst disciplinary records of all time. So, if virtual football matches up to reality, and you get him sent off, it seems only right that you'll get a punishment – just as Sergio does in real life. Yours is to profess your undying love for Manchester United (or Real Madrid, if you're a United fan) online every day for a week, before announcing that you've 'signed a new contract' at your actual club.

Get sent off as Lee Cattermole

The similarly rash Sunderland captain is also liable to go into the referee's book. Get him sent off and you've got to post a detailed argument online over whether you're more of a cat or a mole, and why. Make it good.

Lose to Leicester

Get out-foxed by the Foxes? Uh oh. This one's tricky. If you're defeated by Leicester, who are owned by Thai-led consortium AFI, then you need to learn some Thai phrases of your opponent's choice. One per goal conceded.

Win with Southampton

Smash someone by more than three with the Saints? Good work but, uh oh, the big boys were watching - and they're bound to poach your stars. Replay the match minus your goalscorers, and see how well you get on then.

Lose to Villa

Aston Villa boss Tim 'Tactics' Sherwood is known for his disdain for the complexities of the game. Get a tonking by his virtual side? Then your opponent gets to choose your tactical setup for the rematch. Like Tim, you can leave all that to someone else.

Get Joey Barton sent off

You wouldn't be the first. But there's a punishment for this one if your team - Burnley, presumably, unless your England side has had an injury crisis - gets beaten by three goals or more, too. Respond to the dismissal by posting five quotes from philosophers on your social media pages.

How FIFA revolutionised the trading cards phenomenon

For football fans of a certain age, there is a certain nostalgia around school lunch breaks spent on the playground, swapping football stickers and trading cards with friends, determined to complete their collections. In Britain, the Panini and Merlin sticker albums became a cult craze, with the frenzied desire to fill up these catalogues dominating the childhoods of many schoolboys.

However, as the digitisation of the late Nineties and beyond took hold, football stickers fell by the wayside, seemingly lost to history, part of a bygone era. Then, for the best part of a decade, they were forgotten about, until the release of *FIFA 09*'s downloadable content, FIFA Ultimate Team – now widely known, simply, as FUT – in March 2009.

But Ultimate Team – or, at least, something similar – had been on the minds of those working at EA Sports from almost the beginning of the series, according to Producer Marc Aubanel, who worked on the game from 1993 to 2002. He says: "The whole manager side of football was something we were talking about from day one. Championship Manager was big at the time, so that was on our radar from the early days – this is not only a great arcade experience, there's a real strategy element too.

"It was just a matter of time until something like FUT emerged. During my tenure, we were just adding teams; logistically, it was pretty much dealing with the new licenses.

"It was always like 'Okay, we've got X new teams, leagues, languages', so we never had the ability to do something like that – we were too busy going to Korea to get their league, etc. But it was inevitable that something like FUT would be a part of FIFA."

The mode had actually first appeared in the Xbox 360 version of *UEFA Champions League 2006–2007*, a special spin-off title from the main *FIFA* game, the separate release necessitated by licensing difficulties with UEFA and FIFA. In order to make the additional game more attractive, other than simply offering Europe's premier cup competition, EA Sports added Ultimate Team, a game mode which allowed users to create their own teams by collecting and trading player cards.

Depending on how their 'collections' – or teams – performed in various matches and competitions, against both the computer and online opponents, the gamer would earn points to add to their squads. Or, if they wanted to go down the Roman Abramovich route, they could purchase card packs using Microsoft Points.

These random selections of cards ranged from 500 points (around £4) for a basic pack, known as Bronze, to 5,000 points for a premier Gold pack. Each contained a variety of players, staff, stadia, kit, and action cards, which all added to the experience – a contract card, for instance, extended the number of games your star man could play for you.

The overall goal of Ultimate Team is to, erm, build the ultimate team, with team chemistry calculated based on nationality, club side, division based in, formation and position, or by being part of the same FUT squad for long enough.

Though, initially, the introduction of FUT was overshadowed by a raft of other improvements – in *FIFA 09*, the novelty of user-controlled celebrations took the initial headlines, followed by a new Live Season mode – it soon established itself as a valuable and innovative part of the game, becoming a series mainstay ever since.

The original Ultimate Team, while not a million miles off, looks basic compared to the modern version.

Not only has it added value to the user experience, it has emerged as a revenue stream for EA Sports, too – one that is remarkably, in many ways, more lucrative than the game itself.

Originally, the game mode was offered as an expansion pack style add-on purchase, costing £10/$10 to bolt onto the main *FIFA* experience – an option taken up by around one million gamers. In the next iteration, *FIFA 10*, it was 30% more popular, and by *FIFA 11,* it was offered as a free download, opened by 3.9 million users, as EA Sports recognised that the money-making value lay in in-game purchases rather than charging for a downloadable content (DLC) pack. From *FIFA 12*, it came as part of the game, integrated onto the disc, with 6.7 million players of the mode, and a confirmed social phenomenon.

A year on and, incredibly, that figure almost doubled, reaching 11.2 million users, as the word continued to spread about the compulsive digital collecting game. Many *FIFA* players were now playing FUT exclusively. The first six months of that game, *FIFA 13*, produced a digital revenue of $200 million, a 94% increase on its predecessor and largely fuelled by FUT – the most popular game mode in EA Sports' most popular game. They'd found the gem for their crown.

Such is the interest, the accompanying iPhone app was amongst the first to be made available for the Apple Watch – for those who want to keep tabs on their team while on the move.

But Ultimate Team's first release, five months after *FIFA 09* came out, was something of an accident. EA had actually been working on the mode with the intention of including it in the release of *Champions League 2009–2010*, a game that never came out, after they decided against renewing the UEFA license.

With the mode half-built, it was an opportunity to offer additional content to the main game, though it meant a lot of work, with the database of Champions League stars, limited to 32 teams, needing to be expanded to include every individual from *FIFA*'s vast pool of players. It was work well worth putting in – by 2013, Ultimate Team had been replicated in each of EA's stable of sports games, including *Madden*.

For Adam Shaikh, Creative Director of FUT, it is a runaway success story that he cannot help but marvel at, having joined the EA Sports team in December 2009, as the first Ultimate Team was being signed off.

Reflecting, he says: "We could always see the potential there – it was very exciting to play. It speaks to you as a football fan – the excitement and hope, the feeling of needing to do something to make your team better: 'if I just get this player, then I'll be ready to take on the world'. From that side, it was always about how do we realise that, and people don't get fed up or bored of it.

"Ultimate Team speaks to a different thought process than, say, Career Mode, which is a little bit more authentic. FUT is not as serious, and things like the transfer market really capture those playground or office conversations, because it is online, you are competing, and you can give advice to each other.

"Even after six years of working on FUT, I still play it on a regular basis, which is rare for a game developer. Usually, by the time you've finished your game, it's hard to maintain that enthusiasm. So, to have made five or six versions and still be really keen on it shows how great an experience it is.

"And it's grown. When we looked at the first one, people played for a few months, the second one people played for six months, so our focus has been on making it fun for the whole year.

"I wouldn't say it's a surprise that people have enjoyed playing it, but the fact that it's now the biggest mode in FIFA obviously is. We couldn't have imagined it would be *the* most popular mode. It's always incredibly exciting to see how popular the game has been year-on-year."

Of course, he's right. Now, with the release of *FIFA 16*, it is arguably the most eagerly anticipated element of the new title – the first time the game disc is put into a games console, its user is more than likely to head straight for FUT and begin building their collection. For many, this will be December 25th, with Christmas money to spend, and three months of catching up to do.

The model of purchasing player packs has now been refined. Bronze packs, the most basic offering on the *FIFA* market, cannot be purchased with cash – these are buyable only by amassing enough Match Coins by playing games. The cheapest pack, which includes twelve cards, one of which is rare, costs 400 Coins – an easily attainable amount (given that playing a solitary FUT match generates several hundred Match Coins).

The exact number is calculated by a fairly lengthy formula – with Coins awarded for various factors, including goals scored (40 per strike, up to 200), keeping a clean sheet (75), and for your pass accuracy percentage (1 per percentage). That total is deducted for goals conceded (20 for each, up to 80), fouls committed (5, up to 20), and being caught offside (1, up to 15).

To further complicate things, your figure is then subjected to a DNF (Did Not Finish) multiplier, designed to punish those who regularly 'rage quit' games when losing, while a completion bonus of up to 325 Coins is payable for seeing out the full tie.

The full Match Coins calculator for *FIFA 15* is illustrated in the table below:

Bonuses	Coins per Unit	Maximum Limit
Scored Goals	40	200
Shots on Target	5(1)	50
Successful Tackles	1	20
Corners	5	50
Clean Sheets	75	75
Pass Accuracy	1	80
Possession	1	80
Man of the Match	15	15

Penalties	Coins per Unit	Maximum Limit
Goals Against	-20	-80
Fouls	-5	-20
Cards	-10	-80
Offside	-1	-15

This means that the cheapest Bronze pack is easily attainable – effectively, one game away from buying. The more premium Bronze offering, which boasts three rare cards compared to one, costs 750 Match Coins.

For Silver level packs, the stakes rise considerably. Its basic offering – 12 cards, including one rare, as with Bronze – costs either 2,500 Coins or 50 *FIFA* Points, the in-game currency which can be purchased with real money. In this instance, two of the 50 FP Silver packs would cost 79p – the price of 100 *FIFA* Points in-game. A 12,000 *FIFA* Point pack, the biggest bundle available, costs £80.

The Silver pack offering three rare cards is priced at 3,750 Coins or 75 Points, while the first Gold pack – which has twelve cards, including one rare and guarantees at least ten of them are Gold cards – requires 5,000 Coins or 100 Points.

The most expensive Gold pack on offer is priced at 7,500 Coins or 150 Points and guarantees the buyer the same deal as the cheaper Gold pack, but with three rare cards.

Special Edition Gold packs are often made available, usually around events such as *FIFA*'s end of season community awards – the FUTties – which introduces a team-of-the-season style line-up of special pink 'in form' cards to the marketplace. For those keen to add these players to their teams and collections, there were two FUTties-specific packs available, including one priced at 25,000 Coins or 350 Points.

As with any currency, there have been issues for EA Sports to contend with, most notably external sites selling Match Coins illegally, undercutting the equivalent cost of official *FIFA* Points, and widely promoted by high-profile, *FIFA*-playing YouTubers – whose fame we explored in Chapter Eight.

This practice emerged out of users who were desperate to add a Cristiano Ronaldo or Lionel Messi to their side, without the hassle of earning enough Coins to purchase them on the FUT transfer market.

Quite rightly, football's two biggest stars are hard to find in a random pack, but signing them from another player is fairly straightforward if you have enough Coins, with eBay style auctions. However, because EA protected the transfer market by making it Coins-only – and, therefore, you couldn't just use real money to buy whoever you wanted – it led to frustrated gamers who weren't willing to actually earn enough for their targets through matches. Eventually, someone caught on to this gap in the market and exploited it by selling the currency – taking payment through PayPal, and then paying well over the odds for a worthless card listed for sale by their customer, safe in the knowledge that no one else would swoop for the over-priced card.

Not only did this play further into the hands of those who wanted to buy their way to success – too impatient now to even buy a pack of random cards – but it also left the transfer market crippled. EA's first reaction to the sudden flooding of the Match Coins market was to introduce set valuation ranges for player sales, intending to maintain a level playing field.

Instead, it allowed stacked players to simply buy up all the top names at knockdown prices – with many stars eventually becoming 'extinct', as they were available at a fixed maximum price, and a bidding war could no longer emerge. Ronaldo, for example, was available for up to 6.2 million Coins. For those not willing to invest real money, one Twitter user calculated that it would require more than 27 weeks of consecutive gaming to earn the required Coins.

The move also removed a key element for innovative gamers who couldn't afford to invest real-world money – 'flipping' players by buying cheap and selling high. It punished the indiscretions of opportunists by penalising the most dedicated managers, who would scour the market at all hours for a bargain.

It meant that, now, the only way to build and develop a FUT squad was to put in hour upon hour of matchplay, or cold harsh cash, and it prompted an online backlash – including the Twitter hashtag #RIPFUT – and a *Guardian* article entitled 'Has EA just broken FIFA Ultimate Team?'

But, to EA's credit, it was an issue that was quickly recognised as something that needed to be addressed, with the proposed solution – beyond clamping down on illicit Coin selling operations – a new FUT element introduced in *FIFA 16*, the Draft.

Described by Adam Shaikh as: "the biggest game-changer we've ever had", it is a four-match mode that allows users to draft a random pool of players from which they can craft a squad. This means that everyone, no matter how much money or time they're prepared to spend on the game, has the same shot at playing with the sport's big guns.

Offered a selection of five cards for each position, randomly generated from across the football world, players can put their side together in whichever way they desire, much like the full FUT game.

Then, with squad selected, gamers play four matches with their line-up, and the results during those games dictate what prize they receive at the end. The minimum amount on offer is equal to Draft's entry fee – paid for through Match Coins, *FIFA* Points, or Draft Tokens, which are attained through *FIFA* Packs – meaning that it's a no-loss situation that cannot be exploited by a heavy wallet.

The new-look FUT Draft mode from *FIFA 16*.

As Shaikh explains: "We wanted to have an opportunity for players to play with stars they don't usually get – how often does the average player get Ronaldo? We spent years building Ultimate Team to be a mode you can play for the entire year but, for some, that's a bit too much commitment. Draft distils the essence of FUT, all the elements of team building.

"We've always tried to be as sympathetic as possible – there's nothing in Ultimate Team that requires micro-transactions anywhere, there's nothing gated or impossible to get. For example, the transfer market is a great way of getting what you want, and you can't use micro-transactions to do that.

"We want to provide a great experience, the best game mode we can possibly do, and if someone wishes to spend something, then they will but we don't push people towards it. It is there, it is part of the game, but our focus isn't on micro-transactions, in terms of how we think about things and build the games.

"As FUT has got bigger, we've had different challenges, things we've had to address that aren't necessarily things we're used to, such as the attempts to make sure we're keeping Coin-selling under control, to make sure we have a fun, fair, secure experience for all of our gamers.

"Obviously, we're not looking at taking more money or exploiting anyone, it's all about trying to make the best game possible."

And, mostly, that standpoint is accepted. Even in a world where micro-transactions are considered somewhat underhand, the Ultimate Team model has been generally accepted, even if there were suspicions about it at first.

Games reviewer Rik Henderson reflects: "It had a rocky start, because it seemed to be devised to make revenue for the game, which is a philosophy that doesn't sit pretty with many people.

"But, actually, FUT is a great, fun mode to play, and it speaks straight to that fantasy football feeling that you can make up your team of legends, and it rewards better play with better players. It's now the biggest mode on FIFA by a long, long, long way."

That popularity means that FUT has almost developed as a game in its own right, separate from the main *FIFA* release – the phenomenal interest in the mode is such that the UK announcement of Draft was accompanied by the release of a short film starring *Sky Sports* pundits Gary Neville and Jamie Carragher playing it. Filmed in former Manchester United defender Neville's living room, the footage reflects the pulling power of the *FIFA* series: Neville and Carragher would be the premier double-act for any football-related content. For any other company, signing them would be a coup – for EA Sports and *FIFA*, it was standard practice and spoke volumes for Ultimate Team's status.

***Sky Sports* pundits Jamie Carragher and Gary Neville
teamed up to reveal FUT Draft.**

Given that it is the most profitable and popular element of the series, Ultimate Team has its own dedicated team working to ensure the mode continues to grow in parallel to its audience.

Adam Shaikh, who heads up that team, offers an insight into how FUT is developed: "It's an organic process. When working on the next version, the first thing we're looking at is what our gamers want and do. People don't always know *what* they want exactly – they often have feelings or responses that we have to take and work out which features will satisfy them.

"We think about things that are already in the game as much as those that aren't, to make sure that things we've done in the past are still valid. Sometimes it's a case of 'we thought this would be a great idea, turns out people don't really like it, so let's reconsider'. Or even things that are working quite well – we go back and say 'if we were making that decision now, would we still make the same decision' because sometimes they're a matter of circumstance. Two years later, the world has changed.

"We don't go from scratch – we still have ideas of great features that we think people will really love – but we will always reassess at the beginning of every project. For example, one of the things we've always put a lot of effort into has been to try to allow people to build in different ways. So, we changed the chemistry system between FIFA 09 and FIFA 10, and that really allowed people to think about how they were going to put together their team.

"Things like Team Of The Week mean that the world is ever-changing, because you thought you were happy with your team, and then suddenly a great player became available. Fortunately for us, we have a very good creative team, so we have so many ideas on how FUT can develop."

And the scope of the FUT team's power and changes has surely expanded rapidly since the mode's emergence – as the most popular and profitable area of *FIFA*, Adam and his team must feel like a key cog in the game's system… EA Sports' very own Cristiano Ronaldo. Not that they acknowledge it, or expect preferential treatment akin to what the Portuguese superstar demands at Real Madrid. Shaikh says: "Just because it's the most popular mode, that doesn't necessarily mean it's a priority or main focus. Because FIFA is such a big game, there are so many people that play so many parts. So my particular focus is very much on Ultimate Team – that's what me and my team do – but there is a Career Mode team, and all the teams that work on the other modes. It's not as if there's nothing else.

"But Ultimate Team has grown rapidly. At one point, I used to know all the numbers, in terms of players and popularity, but it's so big now that there's far too much going on to worry about that."

Shaikh's appraisal of FUT's popularity is modest – the mode has proved to be a revelation, spawning its own community of diehards and enthusiasts, all interacting on a daily basis, comparing notes – and teams – as they compete to have the best Ultimate Team, however they might define it.

It's this activity that Rob Hodson – EA's Social and Community Manager – monitors day to day, marvelling at the passion and the breadth of the audience that interacts with each other online about FUT.

He says: "Ultimate Team has, by far, the biggest online presence in terms of conversation. It's pretty straightforward as to why – knowledge is power, in the sense that if you know ways to trade, when to buy things, when to sell things, then you progress significantly in the game.

"So there is a distinct benefit of you participating in the community. Whether that's on an official forum or just through your Twitter or watching YouTubers, you gain an advantage by being part of that. It's not just a one-way thing, where you come on and take, you get from putting into it as well. Ultimately, that's what everyone's in for – getting towards the Ronaldos and Messis and superstar teams.

"There are FUT players who take it very seriously. We have people on the forum who make it a point to buy every player of a certain team, of a certain type; we have people who just collect the bronze players, who never touch silver or gold.

"And they talk for hours on end on the forums, just about these players. Some people just want the very best clubs and players, we have leaderboards for the club size, and there are people that make an effort to collect every single player in the game, which is going some. There are people taking it very seriously, but definitely not all for the same reason.

"Some people just want to play rather than collect. The actual make-up of their teams is just a means to an end. For example, there's a guy at the moment who plays on PlayStation, and he has 2050 wins, 86 losses and 142 draws, which is a 90% win rate over 2278 matches.

"Which is quite incredible and also something he clearly takes seriously, but in a different way from the people who are focused on collecting. It's quite a personal thing."

One of the key developments in the FUT community is the emergence of partner websites such as *FUTWIZ.com*. Co-founded by Dan Bellis, a former competitive gamer, it acts as a database of players, tracking their fluctuating price tags.

The idea came from his own gaming experiences, as a fan himself. Bellis says: "I've always been a FIFA gamer, since the first iteration. I used to play FIFA competitively, going into tournaments while I was at university, on FIFA 09, 10 and 11.

"Then I left Uni and went into full-time employment; I wanted something more casual to play, so I started getting into the Ultimate Team mode. But, still being the competitive player that I was, I got heavily into FUT.

"I took the same attitude from pro gaming into it – playing lots of games, trying to make the best possible squads, which then got me involved in the EA FIFA community forums, where I met Ruan Holder. It was in this community that FUTWIZ was created.

"Originally, Ruan coded up a small website to make realistic looking FUT items with custom stats to troll me. My favourite player at the time was Nicklas Bendtner – he played for Sunderland, the team I support – and he would make awful Bendtner items that looked authentic, just to mock me.

"From that, we decided to make it into a tool that everyone else could use. And that became a squad builder that then became a database site. It turned out quite a lot of people quite liked using it."

That's a slight understatement – in 2014, both Dan and colleague Ruan had left their day jobs to work full time on the site, as it generated enough income through advertising to be a viable business.

So why does Dan think his site – and FUT in general – is so popular? Because it feeds into football fans' obsession with facts, stats and opinions: "The FUT community has an incredible attention to detail. Because FUT goes hand-in-hand with real life, there's discussion all the time, there's never really a dull moment.

"People are discussing who could get an 'in form' item in Ultimate Team. There are discussions and arguments and fallings out over who they think deserves it, who's better than who, because only 18 players get those items per week. That prompts a very heated and passionate discussion. It's a very dedicated community.

"It's been a meteoric rise for Ultimate Team. Year on year it just seems to be getting bigger. As more people get introduced to the mode, I think Draft will make things more accessible for players who just want to pick up and play for an evening, and a lot less daunting, so FUT will just keep on growing."

He's well placed to judge, as an active part of the community, and Dan uses that insight to explain something that outsiders often find difficult to understand – why people spend real money on a virtual game: "When I was a FUT player I spent a fair amount of my student loan on it – not an obscene amount but, sometimes, rather than going out and having a few beers, I'd open a few packs on Ultimate Team instead.

"A lot of it is one-upmanship and the ability to brag when you've got something. If they see someone with Ronaldo in their team, they'll want Ronaldo too, so they open some packs.

"For the type of people who play and pay, it's a hobby – they play in the evening or on their days off. Instead of going out for a meal, sometimes they'll sink a few quid into FIFA. Some of the hardcore players probably spend up to £100 a month.

"It seems ludicrous to say you've spent that amount of money on a game but, when you compare it to the amount of time you've spent on it, you actually get a lot out of that. People will play hundreds of FIFA matches over the course of the year so, really, for per minute enjoyment, it's not really that expensive."

That vast and wide-ranging appeal has, not surprisingly, inspired *FIFA* to pursue online gaming options – the likes of which we explored in Chapter 7 – for their flagship mode in the game, Ultimate Team.

Indeed, the Play Like a Legend Championships, hosted by *Gfinity* and *Microsoft* in 2015 in the weeks before the release of *FIFA 16*, was the first time an exclusively Ultimate Team tournament had been held. Previously, in the likes of *FIWC*, tournaments used the Head-to-Head mode.

With a £6,420 prize pool on offer at the end of each season, there's a Grand Final to determine who takes the winner's cheque of just over £3,000. The inaugural champion was French gamer KVega who beat Brit player Samba1889 5-4 in the final, after emerging from 39 finalists to lift the crown.

And, increasingly, the stigma of micro-transactions has dissipated, with FUT emerging as a valuable bonding tool for parents and teenage sons – something Ben Williams, 31, from Birmingham, has found.

He said: "I've played Ultimate Team from the start. I play with my kids. It was such a fresh concept for a video game that it just grabbed me – it was so unique. It took me back to collecting trading cards and stickers at school; that kind of mentality. I was determined to complete all of the collections.

"It was FIFA 12 when I started spending a fair amount on the game, and it's evolved with each release since. I have no problems in spending a bit of money at the start of a new release.

"For FIFA 15, I spent about £800 upon release, to give us a bit of a head start, and then around £25 per week after. Which, to me, is the same as going to the cinema if there's something on we want to watch.

"When the kids were collecting football cards, it didn't cost much less to fund things – you'd waste hundreds chasing one particular card. FUT is year-round and we play it all the way through until the next edition, so that's almost twelve months it keeps us occupied for. It's great value for money."

*

As Ultimate Team continues to come into its own, it's little surprise that the new FUT element, Draft, was one of the headline features teased by EA Sports when unveiling *FIFA 16*. In the next chapter, we'll look at the latest edition in greater detail, and how it will attempt to be the finest *FIFA* yet…

The Ultimate Dream Team
How FIFA wades into the 'greatest ever' debate

The addition of Legends to Ultimate Team offers an intriguing way of comparing football's greatest players in history – given the depth of detailed statistics that goes into rating a player numerically in the game. Here, we feature some of the classic players added to the game, and how they were rated in comparison to today's stars. For reference, in *FIFA 15*, Lionel Messi was rated as a 93, and Cristiano Ronaldo 92, on release.

Moore love for Bobby? West Ham great ranks alongside the best ever defenders.

Win back: Carlos is crowned top left wing back in this face-off.

Great Danes: Schmeichel tops the Laudrup twins, according to *FIFA*.

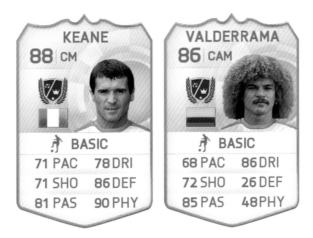

An intriguing midfield partnership: short fuse meets big hair.

One Al of a front-line: this triple threat spells goals.

10. Allow me to introduce you to the newborn King – FIFA 16

What to expect from the latest instalment of the FIFA series

So, having reflected on the past of the series, what about the present – what does the current edition, *FIFA 16*, hold for us? Having played the rest, we're now ready for the best, and EA Sports have rarely disappointed us in the past.

They promise us 'innovation across the entire pitch' in gameplay, with massive changes in every position affecting the way we'd got used to playing *FIFA*. As the series has taught us in the past, you're never comfortable for long. A bit like a player in possession against Barcelona.

The UK cover of *FIFA 16* – with Liverpool's Jordan Henderson alongside Lionel Messi.

One of the main focuses of *FIFA 16* has been the next stage in levelling the playing field, literally, between defence and attack – with the gradual balancing of the two reaching its peak here. While wingers have, for years, been dynamic to control, with freestyle dribbling

172

options and fancy flicks and tricks and the like, now defenders have caught up with Defensive Agility. Driven by more than 25 gameplay feature changes to defender locomotion, it means that the player on the back-foot, too, can be flexible now, and can adjust to changing pace and direction. Regaining possession should be as fluid as rampaging forward with it.

The AI of the backline has also been improved, meaning that, when defending, the player you're controlling won't be abandoned by his peers, who have been known to make curious choices in recent history. Your other defenders will be better equipped to gauge whether they should mark the lethal forward wandering free – yes! – and when they should move into potentially dangerous space.

New behaviours added to the game include fake and standing tackles, full-body challenges, and the ability to pull out of a sliding tackle when caught out of position. No longer does one wrong move leave your defence parting like the Red Sea for Moses. Which should also up the ante for the kick-off game – if you don't play it, scoring direct from the kick-off counts double, and happened fairly often in previous iterations. Sliding tackles are now less 'last resort', and more a nuanced tactical decision.

In the middle of the park, an area that has previously felt bypassed in recent series entries – get the ball wide and forward and you're set, was the common approach. Two savvy new additions to gameplay should help re-establish the engine room as the battlefield. If that isn't too many metaphors for you to keep track of.

The first allows for more precision and purpose when your playmaker gets on the ball, with the all-new driven pass – allowing for sharp, incisive passing that can unlock opposition defences, and find teammates accurately. It's the sort of probing that Barcelona and Bayern Munich excel at in real life, and is a welcome addition to *FIFA*.

FIFA 16 will allow gamers to defend like Chelsea's resolute title winning side of 2014/15.

Secondly, for the more cautious midfield man – which virtually every team, in an era of 4-5-1, seems to have – improved AI has radically bolstered interceptions, with players now closing down passing channels far more intuitively, rather than backing off haplessly until you took control of them. Similarly, midfielders will drop in to cover for defenders caught out of position – which, if you had David Luiz in your team, could be a recurring problem in recent iterations.

But, if those sound like major changes, *FIFA* still remains true to its attacking roots – it is a video game, after all – with what the marketing bods in EA Towers have dubbed 'moments of magic'.

These two new elements give further impetus to dangerous players on the ball, whether their threat is beating you in a one-on-on on the sideline, or from the six-yard line. No Touch Dribbling allows for creativity to prosper without a script or, indeed, boot – players can buy space and time by feinting, dummying, and stepping over the ball.

A feature inspired by Lionel Messi's motion capture sessions, it means that switched on gamers can make the most of over-eager defenders, and create that vital half-yard for themselves without even touching the ball. Simply by pressing and holding the L1/LB button, you'll see your player step away from the ball momentarily to generate some space – then, flicking the lift analog stick allows you to shift your player's body in several directions to fool the defender into sliding in rashly, as you sprint past.

And a new shooting option has been added, with Clinical Finishing adding yet more variety in dispatching the ball towards the onion bag. It can make for some glorious, long-range firecrackers, or some embarrassing efforts ballooned closer to the corner flag. Both of which are seen on a typical game day. The idea is that players will aim to produce more of an angled finish, by wrapping their foot around the ball. If there's no angle to generate, you'll end up embarrassing yourself, if there is, you could be in for a sweetly-struck screamer.

Messi's gliding, dribbling style influenced a brand new feature for *FIFA 16* – No Touch Dribbling.

With so much going on, EA Sports have been keen to ensure that no one gets left behind – unveiling the *FIFA* Trainer system, which coaches you as you play. As you improve, so too does the advice – allowing for more advanced skills and features once you've mastered the basics.

Using a graphical overlay that displays the options in each scenario, with labelled controls making it easy to decipher, players can rehearse and master certain sequences of play. It won't be for everyone, and can be switched off, but the Trainer mode promises to be an inclusive and useful option for those who wish to improve.

Santiago Jaramillo, Producer on the game, believes that it's a key addition, especially to attract yet more players to the series. He said: "Our core fans buy the game and play it and know how to. But so many people want to get into FIFA, but it is a complicated game – and playing online can be very intimidating. There are a lot of people that don't play.

"So the Trainer came up as an idea to give you hints at what you can do in certain situations. Not saying what you should do now, but an on-screen semi-contextual button hint. It's mainly a way to teach people how to play the game in a way that is not intrusive, and doesn't require you to go into a new mode exclusively to do that. You can play how you want to play, and have that guide. When the game recognises that you do things well, it sees that you're progressing, and teaches you new things."

*

Women's national teams take the field for the first time in the series in *FIFA 16*.

The headline change for *FIFA 16*, of course, is that 12 women's national teams will feature for the first time in franchise history – with Australia, Brazil, Canada, China, England, France, Germany, Italy, Mexico, Spain, Sweden and the USA all represented across various modes.

As ever, EA's timing was impeccable – the announcement made before the FIFA Women's World Cup captured the imagination of viewers around the world, who lauded the standard of play. In England, the nation got behind the Lionesses as they finished in an unexpected third place, bolstering attendances at subsequent league matches back home. The Women's FA Cup final drew a crowd of more than 30,000.

It also came just a year after the expansion of the Women's Super League in the UK, with a second tier added, such is the growing popularity and interest in the female game. With plans to make the division fully professional, *FIFA*'s addition of women's teams to the series couldn't have been more welcome – but it wasn't just a cynical add-on, an afterthought inspired by the success of the World Cup in Canada, right on EA's doorstep. It was actually the culmination of years of work.

Nick Channon, *FIFA 16*'s Senior Producer, explained: "Adding women was one of the most important additions we've ever made in FIFA history – a lot went into it.

"When we announced it, most of the questions were 'why now?' and the simple answer was that it took us quite a while to do it well. We created a prototype for it about three years ago, where we actually had – and never expected to ship it – a female head on a man's body.

"We ran that around, played with the prototype, and wrote down all the things wrong with it. That created a list of all the things we needed to work on, and one of the biggest things was body types – it wasn't convincing. It looked like a female because it had long hair, but it wasn't enough.

"We really felt like we had to rework the way we did body types and body shapes to make it feel more authentic. We wanted to do motion capture, we wanted to make sure we had visually authentic heads so we did a lot of scanning. Even down to the audio – 'he shoots', obviously, is something you can't have. So it was a lot of work, which is why it took us a little while to do it, but we wanted to do it properly."

Part of 'doing it properly' was inviting four of the US national team's biggest stars – Sydney Leroux, Alex Morgan, Megan Rapinoe, and Abby Wambach – to EA Canada to undergo motion capture, with their movement used to build a new locomotion system specifically for women, which includes new walks, run, sprints, and horizontal movement.

Also visiting EA were North American rivals Soccer Canada, who provided full-player references using the 360 degree body scanning rig, from which player models were created. While a mobile head-scanning unit visited various tournaments and events around the world to sweep up additional detail – such as facial features and individual hairstyles, to maximise the level of realism on offer – for the graphical database of the women footballers.

**EA's demand for realism meant that full Motion Capture
was undertaken for the first time for women.**

Legendary American striker Wambach – a two-time Olympic gold medalist and former World Player of the Year, who scored the winning goal in the 2015 World Cup final – was a key coup for EA to get involved with the development. America's all-time record goalscorer – with an incredible tally of 183 international goals from 249 caps, which actually makes her the leading international scorer in football history, irrespective of gender – she was understandably upbeat about her role in the game: "We're all excited to see ourselves in the game, but even more excited to see the reaction from all of the fans, including the fans of our team that maybe wouldn't be expecting something like this.

"I honestly can't believe all of the science and technology behind the game itself, let alone getting us into the motion capture suits and, eventually, into the game."

And her disbelief is understandable – the welcome addition of women's national teams to the series came as something of a bolt from the blue inspired, it seems, by a social media campaign.

In February 2013, female professional footballer Vero Boquete wrote a letter to *FIFA*'s executive producer David Rutter, amongst various EA marketing bods, urging them to "contribute to the equality of women in sport".

She posted it online on campaign website *Change.org*, petitioning EA to add women to *FIFA*, writing: "We can do much to advance equality through sports – I want to contribute through this request.

"It seems silly, but it is not – including players in FIFA encourages girls who, like me, love football, to develop her passion, to compete and normalises the relationship between women and sport. Because kids today are playing adult society tomorrow – let the football help break barriers."

Very quickly, the petition went viral, attracting more than 20,000 signatures within 24 hours. When EA Sports announced that *FIFA 16* would include women's teams, it prompted a joyous statement from Boquete, who had just joined Bayern Munich and captained Spain at the World Cup. She wrote: "This is a major step for the normalisation of women's football. We have created an international movement for equality in sport."

England Lionesses captain Steph Houghton as she appears in *FIFA 16*.

Katherine Sladden, Campaigns Director of *Change.org*, commented: "Female campaigners using Change.org have seen lots of success in the last few years. From Caroline Criado Perez's campaign to keep women on UK banknotes, through to Lindsay Garrett's campaign to save her estate, women are often great storytellers who share more readily on social media.

"Often they will underpin campaigns with personal stories, which really helps to get Change.org users emotionally engaged and give their campaigns momentum. Campaigns such as Vero's make an impact because they manage to bring a big topic like sexism to life

To celebrate new tutorial mode, our top skill moves

One of the biggest new elements introduced in *FIFA 16* is the all-new Trainer mode – an overlay that can 'coach' you to virtual success – offering control prompts at opportune moments and which adjusts to become more advanced as you do. Clever stuff.

Feeling suitably inspired by that, here are some of our favourite skill moves from years gone by – and how to perform them. Whether that's in an exhibition match against the computer, or in the deciding moment of your head-to-head with that mate you struggle to beat.

Of course, sometimes, it's best to just KISS – no, we don't mean get all affectionate with your opponent, although that could work by distracting them, we mean Keep It Simple, Silly.

So there are tricks for beginners, intermediates, and full-on experts. We'll leave you to decide which rank best describes your abilities.

Top Beginner Moves

Body feint

Flick your right stick left or right. Easy! And, at the right moment, very effective.

Foot fake (while standing)

Xbox 360/One: LT (hold) + RB (tap)

PlayStation 3/4: L2 (hold) + R1 (tap)

Each tap is a foot fake. Don't do any more than three, though, as your opponent will soon be onto you, and just tackle you as you fake over air.

Dragback

Xbox: RB + ↓ (flick)

PlayStation: R1 + ↓ (flick)

The van Basten classic. What do you mean you don't know who that is…

Stepover

Flick the right stick in any forward or sideways moving direction (↑, ↖, ← / ↑, ↗, →) to do your best Cristiano Ronaldo impression. Remember, there is such a thing as overdoing it.

Keepy uppies

Xbox: LT (hold) + RB (tap)

PlayStation: LB (hold) + R1 (tap)

Perfect for wasting time in the corner, for taunting your opponent at kick off or, erm, in your own box deep in injury time.

Top Intermediate Moves

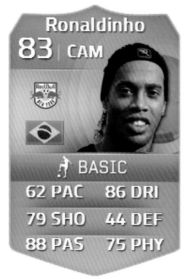

Heel flick

RS ↑, ↓ (flick)

Easy to do, but looks pretty swish too.

Fake left, go right

RS ←, ↙, ↓, ↘, →

Get this one right, and you'll look like Ronaldinho in full flow. Get it wrong, and you'll look like an idiot.

Simple rainbow

RS ↓, ↑, ↑ (flick)

Now we're getting trickier than Run DMC (they were a rap group), but timing this move well can be a flamboyant delight.

Ball roll cut right

RS ←(hold), →(hold)

The bright amongst you will have cottoned onto the fact that you can change this to left by doing it in the opposing direction. The rest of you are still reading this.

Spin left

RS ↙, ↙

Eat my dust, Chris Brown! That's the dance-y R&B singer rather than the Blackburn striker – but either works.

Top Expert Moves

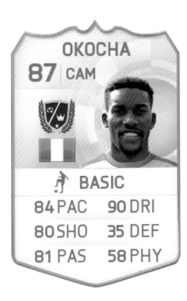

Advanced rainbow

↓ (flick), ↑ (hold),↑ (flick)

Mastered the simple rainbow from the intermediate moves? Get you, flash sausage. Try this one, then, if you're a real hot dog…

Stop and turn while running

RS ↑ (flick), → (flick)

Do this quickly and smoothly. Otherwise you might be disappearing off the sideline.

Triple Elastico

RS ↓, ↘, →, ↘, ↓, ↙, ←

Crikey, this one's got more moves than the Kama Sutra but it looks elastico fantastico when it comes off. One to practice offline before using on your mates.

Rabona flick while jogging

Xbox: LT + X / B, A + ↓

PlayStation: L2 + square/circle, X + ↓

Yeah, this one's beyond me – you're a better *FIFA* player if you can master this. Having watched it on *YouTube*, it looks extraordinary, and almost justifies a sweaty goal after.

Around the world

RS ↓, ↙, ←, ↖, ↑, ↗, →, ↘, ↓ / ↓, ↘, →, ↗, ↑, ↖, ←, ↙, ↓

This one's a juggling move, but it's the classic flick that all wannabe freestyle footballers start with. And still looks every bit as impressive in pixel form.

Done all that? Congratulations, you're on your way to Man City for £1gazillion.

Those joining Messi from overseas

As *FIFA 16* was the first iteration where regional cover stars were decided by popular votes, EA Sports once again produced a savvy engagement method to ramp up the excitement of fans awaiting the new release.

In the UK, newly appointed Liverpool captain Jordan Henderson was selected to appear alongside global cover star Lionel Messi, but his face won't be as prevalent in other territories – where local heroes will instead grace the cover.

Amongst those voted in was former Manchester United playmaker Shinji Kagawa, recent Barcelona signing Arda Turan, and the first three women to appear on the cover.

Big in Japan: How the Japanese version of *FIFA 16* looks.

Mex, next: Marco Fabián of Guadalajara is the Mexican cover star.

Full list of *FIFA*'s cover athletes

- Australia: Steph Catley and Tim Cahill
- Austria: David Alaba
- Brazil: Oscar
- Canada: Christine Sinclair
- France: Antoine Griezmann
- Italy: Mauro Icardi
- Japan: Shinji Kagawa
- Latin America (except Brazil and Mexico): Juan Cuadrado
- Mexico: Marco Fabián
- Poland: Arkadiusz Milik
- Turkey: Arda Turan
- UK and Ireland: Jordan Henderson
- US: Alex Morgan

In the case of Arda Turan, Turkey's choice of cover star, he had to appear in his national team kit – having left Atletico Madrid. His signing for Barcelona cannot be registered until January 2016 due to the Catalan club's transfer ban, leaving him technically temporarily club-less.

The Australian cover (shown in Chapter Ten) is particularly patriotic, with two golden Aussie jerseys visible alongside Messi – partly because Tim Cahill plays for Shanghai Shenhua in the Chinese Super League, a division that isn't licensed for the game. Compatriot Steph Catley, meanwhile, is only playable in the game as part of her international side.

The Pole poll winner was something of a surprise, with Arkadiusz Milik, whose loan at Ajax was made permanent in the summer, beating off stiff competition from the likes of Bayern's Robert Lewandowski, Sevilla's Europa League-winning midfielder Grzegorz Krychowiak, and Arsenal's loaned out goalkeeper Wojciech Szczesny.

There was a far less surprising result in Austria – where national icon David Alaba, the youngest player to play for his country, was chosen. Already a four-time Bundesliga winner at Bayern Munich, Alaba had established himself as one of his country's most successful ever players in his early twenties.

In the UK, of course, Jordan Henderson had started out as something of a dark horse – with sensation of the season Harry Kane expected to win the vote – but, with the power of Liverpool behind him, Anfield's newly crowned leader won out.

11. FIFA future: a gaze into the next generation of video gaming

What to expect from the future instalments of the FIFA series

Given *FIFA*'s remarkable journey – from a Canadian firm's uncertain dabble in football to the greatest and most popular virtual version of the planet's favourite sport – seemingly anything might be possible in the future for the series.

From 2D graphics of generic, pixelated players to hyper-realistic visuals that are recognisably based on intricate headscans of real-world stars; from national squads packed full of random names and those of the staff working on the title to the most thoroughly licensed product in video game history; from calling itself 'soccer' in order to appeal to an American market to taking over the world with jaw-dropping sales figures – you'd almost think that *FIFA* has already reached its pinnacle.

But it would take a brave man or woman to even whisper that suggestion within the halls of EAC, the Vancouver home of EA Sports' range of titles. The driven workforce there are relentless in their pursuit of development and trailblazing. Just as, in the early days, EA refused to get complacent because they'd secured a few, key licenses, now they're not letting their prized product's success dilute their vision.

Everything has to be bigger and better, more realistic, more enjoyable; as football evolves, so too must *FIFA*. It's a mission statement that is taken very seriously.

Certainly, there's scope for EA Sports to be ambitious – as, scientifically, video games are a long way from their full potential, with huge computer advances anticipated in the approaching decades. As the power of the systems and equipment available increases, so too will the options open to the *FIFA* game. In the next five years, it could change dramatically, and be almost unrecognisable come 2020.

Although, year-on-year, it can be difficult to predict what changes each new iteration of *FIFA* will bring, such forward thinking is no problem for Dr Ian Pearson, the renowned futurologist, and inventor of text messaging, whose award-winning work for *Futurizon* has made him a leader in his field.

Boasting an incredible 85% accuracy at the ten-year horizon for his predictions, Dr Pearson's vision for the *FIFA* series is remarkable – and means that fans have much to look forward to. He said: "A lot of people are using Go Pro cameras, and these sorts of things are getting smaller and smaller.

"So if you've got a camera that is so small that it is like an earring stud, or could be worn on a forehead, you could record the video from the players' point of view, in a real game, then the FIFA gamer can recreate that.

"Similarly, we're starting to see electronics that you put onto the surface of the skin, that monitor your blood and heartbeat. The next generation of that might be devices implanted inside the skin itself that can connect to nerves and record the signals associated with various sensations.

"It's only about two megabytes of data per second for your whole hand, which is really not very much in today's IT terms. So you could record those sensations, stick them on the hard drive, and put them into FIFA so you can feel what it's like to be playing in a match.

"Maybe the players are knackered, or they've got a strain in the left leg, or so on. FIFA could let you replay a full sensory experience of being a top Premier League player in an important game.

"Combined with virtual reality, which we've got coming, it'd make a really convincing way of stepping into our footballing heroes' shoes.

"And these sensations could also be used for training purposes – a coach, rather than shouting on the sidelines, can program their plan on the training pitch. Then, FIFA gamers could go through those same drills as part of a training mode, as the next level of realism of becoming a player – 'attending' a Premier League training session through FIFA.

"This sort of content could be offered as an add-on by the club to season ticket holders. If you buy the FIFA extra for your particular team, that'd allow you to play out the strategies your side uses throughout the season. It would be a sort of bolt-on purchase for players and subscribers."

If such future gazing feels a bit distant and ungraspable, Pearson also predicts dramatic improvements in an area that has long been highlighted as possible to improve by those involved in making the game, right back to the very first FIFA release – the in-game AI.

He says: "Artificial Intelligence is coming on in leaps and bounds, and it won't be very long before we've got a games console in our homes that it as smart as humans.

"The PlayStation 4 is two TeraFLOPS, while the human brain is about 1,000. So the PS4 is 500 times less powerful than our brains, but each generation of console improves - so by the time we have the PlayStation 6, they could be as powerful as we are, which will mean super-intuitive matches against the computer.

"The AI will be very fluid and responsive, just like playing against a real team – a much more lifelike opponent, that's able to second guess you and learn how you play, as a result."

It's a vision that will resonate with those working at EAC – who will no doubt be salivating at the mere thought of Dr Pearson's suggestions. With emerging Virtual Reality technology such as *Oculus Rift* and *PlayStation Morpheus*, gaming – and, therefore, *FIFA* – must be ready to dive into a brand new dimension, particularly if the established order of sports gaming supremacy is to be maintained, with *FIFA* top of the tree.

Certainly, no one at EA is getting carried away congratulating themselves on the current generation of graphics, something former Assistant Producer Marc Aubanel demonstrated when asked to assess whether the game had peaked.

He said: "At the minute, it's just an illusion – in terms of how the players walk, balance, turn, dribble, etc. In terms of the hardcore simulation side, we're just not there yet, we're not at a point where we have the CPU speed to simulate that.

"So as long as computers are still getting more powerful, I think there's still infinite growth in terms of what FIFA can do.

"Soon there will be no motion capture or animation, it will all be algorithmic, just mathematically defined biofuel motion. You're seeing that in generated levels in games, so I could easily see generated animation in a sports game like FIFA being massive.

"I think there's decades of innovation, if not more, of where you could simulate what happens in a game more closely to real life. Because right now it is just a magic trick, a sleight of hand – you're being fooled to believe that these pixels are simulating something they aren't.

"So the great thing is that every year it can get better and better. You'll feel it when you play the game, but you won't know why."

And, similarly, games writer Rik Henderson anticipates large strides to be made to the current *FIFA* product: "I actually think that we're coming into an age where people are starting to understand and realise what the next gen consoles are capable of. And what that will introduce is much better graphical fidelity.

"Gameplay probably won't change an awful lot over the coming years, because they have found a very clever way of playing the game that feels natural. But, in terms of graphics, I don't think we're anywhere near where they're going to end up, even in this generation of consoles. If you look at EA's new Need for Speed, it just looks stunning, like real life. They'll move it all over to the Frostbite engine, and you'll see incredible graphical fidelity.

"We're still not quite there, but we'll also be able to have eleven real life players against eleven real life players playing Sunday League football on FIFA. You won't even have to get off the couch on a Sunday morning."

*

While such innovation is obviously very exciting, implementing futuristic tech must be quite a daunting procedure for those who work on the game – as even the slightest change to their beloved *FIFA* can incur the wrath of the fans.

But for anyone at EA trying to gauge initial reactions – which can be headstrong and hyperbolic – it often pays to ignore all feedback for the first couple of weeks, judging by Senior Producer Nick Channon's experiences: "The first week, people are like 'this is really different' because they're not used to it. Then, after about two weeks, it changes to 'I'm used to this, and it's this I don't like'. So we have to listen to feedback over time."

While any *FIFA* furore is often split into two camps, as Jonathan Pile, the award-winning games journalist for *ShortList Magazine* observes: "There are two things people tend to complain about with any new FIFA: that it's not different enough, or that it's been changed so much that it's completely broken. Obviously, both can't be true – and, in reality, neither are.

"Every new edition has many gameplay tweaks and improvements, most of them behind the scenes, all enhancing how it plays overall. And, by the time we get two games on, the improvement is vast to the point of being nearly unrecognisable as the same franchise.

"And the (frequent) claim that the game is broken? No – it's just different, and players get used to it. Then most can't go back. Sure, there will be some post-release balancing issues but, these days, what game doesn't have that?

"This year, with FIFA 16, is no different, but what else it's added goes beyond mere gameplay tweaks because, for the first time, women's football is included. This is neither a small undertaking in terms of workload, nor one that should be dismissed as a mere PR exercise. The women's game needs exposure to grow in popularity – TV and newspaper coverage will help, but a video game that will sell in the region of five million copies worldwide in its first week is going to make a huge difference for the sport's reach.

"And, now all those stats and player models have been included, their position in the franchise can only grow."

*

For Chip Lange, formerly Product Manager on *FIFA* during the series' infancy, the game has progressed dramatically since his time working on it – when it struggled and strived for legitimacy.

Now, though, he thinks the job is no less difficult, with huge big picture thinking to be done as the radically different gaming industry continues to accelerate in popularity across popular culture – with companies like EA Sports needing to hold on and keep up.

He said: "When we started out, back then, we were going after that sweet-spot niche, the 18- to 24-year-old male video gamer. Gaming hadn't become the largest form of entertainment on the planet at that time, we were just constantly battling with a chip on our shoulder – we felt like we'd won if ESPN would even call us back. We were this little rag-tag group of sports guys from an industry that was thought of as geeks.

"Now you see the referees wear our logos on their sleeve, we're part of a global phenomenon – there are more hours logged on FIFA than watching real sports. We've just become a legitimate part of the sports culture and fabric. When we were tiny, we were fighting for competitive and market validation – now we're the big dog, so everyone targets you.

"And the marketing team working on FIFA now suddenly have global targets – like how do we get it into China? Plus there's a whole other challenge over the next few years: How do we take advantage of the fact that everybody is carrying a games system – a mobile phone – in their pocket? And how do we make FIFA every bit as good as we have on the Xbox One or PlayStation 4? The great thing about this industry is that there's always a new challenge every year."

Whatever happens, you can be sure that future iterations in the *FIFA* series will be made with the same zeal, ambition and obsessive attention to detail that has established the game we know and love as the greatest on the planet.

If there are to be rival franchises that emerge to challenge EA Sports, they will have to be going some to take on the undisputed ruler of the sports video game market – the one thing we can be sure of is that the already blurred line between animation and reality will continue to fade, as *FIFA*'s thirst for realism continues.

And Matt Prior, the man who dreamt up Ultimate Team for the series, believes that plenty more innovation is imminent. He said: "We've got big plans for FIFA. There is a definitive plan of what to do, and where to take it, and I think people will be incredibly excited when that starts to roll out.

"We never run out of ideas, we've got laundry lists of things we want to do, we're perfectionists, we're football fans so there's always somewhere we feel we can take the game. Next year is going to be a big year for us in that respect. Rest assured, the future is bright for FIFA. There are some big ideas coming through soon."